'When I'm in love, it will be forever, I gave you
my heart forever and ever'
- Chris Norman 'No arms can ever hold you'.

A guidebook without pictures, but an inside
view. The story of an island that has my heart.

Rough Diamond Island

This is the really rough guide to the Diamond Isle. A cross between an alternative travel guide and an
autobiography, it will show you the island in a way that most guidebooks wouldn't dare. Thankfully it is not big
book, only 30,000 words are needed to give you a tour of the island from the viewpoint of a sparky and cheeky
around the island walker, followed by the experiences of living here, and a rough guide to island attractions.

Contents

Introducing the Author.

The author is 37 years old, but much younger in mind. She wrote this book while sitting in a wooden house in the mountains during Christmas 2018. The book took less than a week, with the author taking regular breaks to swat flies, feed the animals and do the housework. As well as watching films while she wrote.

This is the author's 20-somethingth book, and she doesn't count them. It is one of the shortest as well as her first travel style book to be published, although she has other travel works in the making, and also belongs to a group of travel writers who review hotels and districts.

The author is female and diagnosed with high-functioning autism, although she doesn't believe a word of that. She also has a broken spine and PTSD, but that is nothing to boast about. She is a fast reader and writer despite having no formal schooling (as you may be able to tell from the writing style).

She spent her career in farming and gardening with very little prospect of leaving the land-based industries until the broken spine diagnosis, when she branched out into freelance writing, and now enjoys the perfect balancing act of writing while caretaking properties and animals, as well as doing some gardening and smallholding work. Spare time hobbies include music, photography, films, and human rights activism. Yes, really.

The Isle of Wight was one of the author's numerous homes, and she retains a great affection for it, keeping in touch with news and issues there from afar.

My Island.

This is the story of my former home, the Isle of Wight. Told through the eyes of an island resident and walker rather than a professional travel writer, so this will tell you more about the real life of the island rather than just the outside view, the tourist view. I got to see the island as a walker, worker, volunteer, resident, curious explorer, writer and photographer.

I often dream of my island, Usually the island in my dreams is peacefully sleeping in the cold winter's night out on the Solent, sometimes the sun shines on the cliffs above Sandown Bay, sometimes the fog is skimming and trailing over Compton Bay. Sometimes I walk Tennyson Down in the silence and beating rain. I dream of my island, with sorrow held at arm's length and reality firmly grasped, but I pray that one day I will walk those shores again in peace, as I did on that first Great Walk.

The book is my island with me forever in my heart. As I wrote this book, I was back on the island in my mind throughout. I was there in every way but physically, and I wanted to stay. I hope for a day when I can return, even just for a while, As I wrote this book, during Christmas 2018, I listened to Chris Norman's Christmas song, and remembered my Christmases on the island, the realities of poverty and the bad health and social systems, and the joy of friends and community at Christmas. Sorrow was at arm's length as reality and practicality leave me here for good reasons and I feel close to my island even at this distance.

This isn't your normal tourist guidebook or informative book on island historic and interesting sites, I won't even launch into rambles over the history, because if you find yourself interested in the island, there is so much information already available to look up. What this is, is the inside view, from someone who walked here, lived here, and loved the island as a whole, problems and delights. It will give you a more rounded view. If you are considering a holiday or buying a home here, don't be put off, be inspired, the island is lovely in its core, it's just that I don't gloss over its very real problems.

The island has significant problems with poverty, education quality, medical services and social and wellbeing care for the vulnerable. But it is home and loved by rich and poor, well and suffering alike. One view of the paradox is to remember two recent events, a mainland politician causing outcry by calling the island a 'Poor White Ghetto', while islanders fiercely stood up to him in response, while at the same time the island won a tourism award for being the most family friendly holiday destination.

This book was drafted freehand without any use of reference sources, purely my experience and memories. I used various sources of reference including friends on the island clarifying points for me before I proceeded with the final draft and publishing the book.

A practical description of the Island. (The boring facts).

The Isle of Wight, a roughly diamond-shaped island off the south coast of the UK (Affectionately known to some as Wight Diamond), is said to be the largest and second-most populated island in Britain, with approximately 141,000 permanent residents last count, although the population swells considerably from that in the summer. The island is 148 square miles in area and the island's motto is 'All this Beauty is of God'. A thought that I often echoed on my round the island walks. It is, in its way, remarkably beautiful. And as described by some guidebooks, the changing scenery of the island is indeed like Great Britain in miniature.

The Isle of Wight is only a few miles from the UK mainland, described as approximately four miles by one source, and two to five by another, the distances vary depending on where you are on the coast and what angle you use.
On a spring tide it looks as if you can walk and swim from Ryde to Portsmouth over the sand, but don't be tempted. Someone I knew earned the headline of trying to walk on water. The hovercraft can run on sea as well as land, but people can't. The Solent is a deep and busy shipping lane, don't swim it, however bad the ferry prices are, unless you have a planned sponsored swim with a guard boat. The great tidal sands at Ryde are good for low water fishing, however.

The island has a history of defence of the mainland from invaders, going back to Carisbrooke Castle being built to ward off the Spanish Armada, and the Island has a long history of being governed by the mainland, but is now a Ceremonial County in its own right, with its own Lord Lieutenant. The island shares a police force with the mainland, and although controversial talks have been had about having a combined authority with the mainland, and also a combined fire service, those plans have been shelved for now. The Isle of Wight likes to be independent, no matter how much bickering reputedly goes on at County Hall in Newport. The local MP is Conservative, and the island has had a Conservative MP since the dark ages.

The Diamond Isle is considered to be very well connected to the mainland, with three car ferries, two fast passenger ferries and a hovercraft. Many islanders complain about ferry prices, which is understandable. Sometimes you could cross the English Channel for less than the price of a car ferry to the Isle of Wight, I have done so.

The ferries are also often disrupted by bad weather such as fog and rough seas in high winds. Unfortunately, this has led to a push for a fixed link between the island and the mainland by bridge or tunnel, which has caused divisions and fears for the island's natural beauty and landscape being ruined.
As yet there is no practical way for a fixed link to be created without causing additional problems for the island and mainland, including disrupting the busy shipping lane, and congestion. The South Coast conurbation that runs parallel with the island has major congestion issues in the same way as the island does.

Sailing is a popular way to visit, with many sailors from the south coast and further afield visiting the island and contributing to its economy as well as keeping the shops at Cowes posh.
There is a bus network run by Southern Vectis, with most routes radiating out from Ryde and Newport, the largest towns. It also has a short railway line between Ryde and Shanklin, overseen by the South's rail network, South Western Trains.
There are main roads between the towns on the island. Until recently the roads of the island had fallen into disrepair, but the local roads contractors, Island Roads, have done extensive work to repair and resurface them.

There are two small airports on the island, for private flights and not commercial ones, these are at Sandown and Bembridge.

The island is a commuter island for some. Combined train and ferry tickets are available, and some workers commute to the south coast or even London for work. The island has some industry but unemployment tends to be high, there are many small enterprises and the usual retail, industrial and commercial sectors. The main industries are agriculture and tourism, with a majority of the island being agricultural land, and over 2 million visitors to the island every year. There is work in ship building and aeronautics, various industrial and commercial work, and work in tourism, a lot of which is seasonal.

There are also emergency services, teaching, medical and council positions as well as a lot of prison positions. Joking aside the island has two prisons, originally three, which I think have now combined, and they house serious and sexual offenders. The prison housing estates are extensive either side of the main road out of Newport towards Cowes. And as a delivery driver I have to comment that the state of the roads on those estates is really bad!

The local hospital, St. Marys, has a high turnover of temporary staff, and rooms are often advertised in Newport as suitable for hospital staff. The island is very reliant on the air ambulance to fly patients with acute conditions to the mainland hospitals at Portsmouth and Southampton as St. Marys is limited in the scope of what it can treat, as I found out when I got poison in my eyes.

The island is divided by more built up areas in the north and east and more rural areas from the south to the west. Most of the island towns are on or near the coast, with Newport slightly inland but still a port via the river medina. There are three rivers, which may once have divided the island, the Medina in the centre, running to the estuary at Cowes, a tidal river. And the Eastern and Western Yar, also tidal and a flood risk, crossing the east and west of the island. There are several lines of Downs, one runs from Culver Down and Cliffs back inland to Newport, the other runs out west of Newport, down to Tennyson Down and the Needles.

The island is known for its sandy beaches, Ryde and Appley, Sandown Bay, Gurnard, Totland, Compton Bay, and more. The bays are what attract large numbers of visitors and day trippers from the mainland. The Isle of Wight gets the prevailing weather and tides, while it protects the South coast at Portsmouth and Southampton and in between, which is why the mainland has shingle beaches while the island's beaches are ground down to fine sand.

Named as the most haunted island, ghost tours are offered, Appuldurcombe House at Wroxall and God's Providence House in Newport are said to be haunted, but in my time on the island I saw no evidence of haunting of any kind, even when I slept in Bembridge Churchyard, shh! I think I scared the ghosts away.

There is plenty of wildlife on the island. Badgers are very common, and there are foxes and deer, as well as rare birds and the usual rodents and rodent-eaters. A recent return of the rare Bittern to nest on the island was joyfully greeted by wildlife lovers. The Military Road cliffs are a popular bird watching venue, as is Newton Creek. And the island is blessed with a very special resident, the Red Squirrel.

Due to being an island, the grey squirrels never arrived here, and the reds dominate. It would be illegal to bring a grey squirrel to the island, so if you are considering it, don't, send it to kennels while you are over. There is a good Red Squirrel charity on the island for information and advice if you want to know more or where to see them. As a gardener I am lucky to often have seen them while I worked. Not so lucky that they didn't like my bonfires and aimed nuts and other projectiles at my head! Believe me, those reds have character and intelligence.

I had better end the boring facts about the island as it detracts from the living and breathing community that my book describes.

Wight Walking.

I will start by retracing the steps of my first walk round the island for charity before I moved there, and will show the island to you as I walk. So please join me on a clockwise walk around the island, and please excuse my rambling, sic. My first walk was clockwise, but in the following walks in the years afterwards, they tended to be anti-clockwise.

I first got to know the Isle of Wight when I decided to do a solo sponsored walk around it for charity...in December and camping out on the way round! What I saw of the Island on that walk I decided me that wanted to live there.

I followed the route that many charity walkers and runners follow, round the perimeter of the island on the official coast path. What many don't find out until they are walking is that the coast path often has closures due to mud or cliff erosion and in places you also have to walk on the road where there is no footpath, so it is a longer walk than the 68 miles advertised. But it is a glorious walk, and with the changing landscapes, it is like walking round a miniature of Great Britain. And since that first walk, I have walked the island a number of times for charity.

When I arrived to walk the island, I landed in Ryde, a town that looks very pretty from the sea, spread out over a hillside with brightly painted houses running down to the golden beaches, and with the several church spires which are Ryde's hallmarks on images and in pictures.

Ryde has been a popular seaside resort at least since Victorian times. The beaches are extensive and sandy and stretch out for a long way on low tide, it is ideal for children's activities, rock pooling and even low water fishing, and there are plenty of cafes and kiosks in the area for refreshments and sunbed hire or water play equipment.

When you arrive by fast catamaran as I did, you have the choice of walking the very long Victorian pier from the catamaran to shore, and enjoying the sea and landscape, or getting the train. The island's trains are, at the time of writing, still old underground trains, distinctive dark red and absolutely bone shaking, although the seats are comfortable. It is quite exciting to ride the train along the pier, especially in wild weather. Island visitors love it.

The trains run from the pier head where the boat comes in, to Shanklin, where there is a connecting bus to Ventnor. The train stops at Ryde Esplanade, St. John's road in the heart of Ryde's residential area, Smallbrook junction to connect with the steam railway, the village of Brading, Sandown for the glorious golden bay, Lake, a residential area of Sandown on the cliffs, and finally the quieter beach and cliff town of Shanklin. The Island Line railway is at the time of writing, run by Southwestern Trains and UK national railcards are valid for any tickets. The railway's main ticket and information office is at Ryde Esplanade, although other stations also have ticket facilities and part time information services.

From Ryde, I followed the coast path clockwise on that first walk. Walking down the esplanade past the small harbour for domestic and fishing vessels, and alongside the sea, past the historic Appley Tower, which is built into the sea wall, looking out to sea and facing a large sandy beach, Appley Beach, which is extremely popular for sunbathers, sports, dog walking and children's activities.

Appley Tower was built in 1875 by local architect William Hutt, as a watch tower associated with a local manor house, Appley Manor, which is now an upmarket restaurant set back some way from the sea (And which does awesome Christmas dinners! I have had dinner there).

Onwards from Appley, this smooth and scenic walk became one of my favourites on the Island, down to Seaview. I did this walk or bike ride along the smooth and even seafront from Ryde to Seaview many times, alone or with others, in my years on the island, no two days are the same, clam seas, rough seas, sunshine or wind and rain, it is beautiful, and throughout your journey, your view across the Solent to the mainland, Portsmouth, Hayling and down towards Chichester, is stunning. Often there are ships and boats on the Solent to be admired, especially the big cruise ships from Southampton. There are weekend days when three cruise ships depart Southampton in convoy, and the locals turn out to watch them.

Out in the Solent are several old forts, complete with weaponry and all the trimmings, but which have been converted to luxury hotels. They are very unique, hotels in the middle of the sea, reachable by helicopter or boat. I know a number of islanders who have spent Birthdays or anniversaries out there, and I can imagine that being stranded out in the middle of the channel in the dark with the sea hitting the side of the fort and the ships going by must be very special. The forts are also used for Weddings and other functions. They have spa facilities and function rooms, bars, and outdoor areas where you can enjoy the view.

My walk took me to Seaview, a small and very exclusive town, best known as a second homes area for wealthy Londoners and their boats, as well as a place for keen and learning sailors. Seaview has a nice little café looking out on the sea, and many walks I was on from Ryde to Seaview would stop at this café for a drink and a cake. But on that first walk round the island, it was late evening and the café was closed.

There are two ways of continuing the round the island walk from Seaview, and it depends on the tide. It is possible to walk along the 'Duver' path from Seaview to St. Helens on a low or ebbing tide, but on a full or incoming tide it isn't possible. You round the corner from Seaview and walk Priory Bay, past the lovely tranquil and exclusive hotel out there. The beach is totally underwater on a high tide, and from the beach you go up onto the path along Bembridge Harbour. I have on other occasions dared the tide and nearly got caught, don't risk it.

On my first walk it was dark and the tide was in, so I walked through Seaview, past the small Grace Church offshoot and the small Anglican church, through Nettlestone and down the dark lane to St. Helens. St Helens is a little village like Seaview, but is more for locals than second-homers. In December, St Helens lights up, with villagers creating angels of all sorts and putting them on display in the village, a special local custom. I got to see the cheery Christmas tree and the angels as I walked that first walk. Numerous communities on the island have a local Christmas tree on the green, which is lovely, Nettlestone, St. Helens and Binstead are some that I can think of.

The next step if you walk through the villages, is down the hill to Bembridge Harbour. Bembridge Harbour is a hub of sailing and also sail training in its sheltered waters looking out onto the English Channel on the corner of the Solent.
But Bembridge Harbour has a surprising visitor attraction. Houseboats, a long row of them. Some are residential, some are holiday lets, and some are known as 'Floatels' floating guest houses. Some of the boats have been neglected in the past and there have even been sinking's. The houseboats are stunning, and you walk right past them on the footpath into Bembridge.

Hidden behind dunes at the end of the harbour is sandy beach, going round to Bembridge's iconic lifeboat station, which is set in the sea, reachable by a long bridge. The lifeboat station opens to the public and you can learn interactively about the lifeboats there and view them. Well worth a visit.

Outside the harbour, on the sea, is St. Helen's Fort, normally surrounded by sea, but several times a year, the lowest spring tides expose a pathway to the fort, and in the summer hundreds of local people follow the ebb tide out to the fort, often with picnics, and enjoy time on the fort before coming back before the incoming tide.

The other side of the road from the harbour is wild marshland, with a waterway for boats to go inland on the river Yar, with the water controlled by locks and drains.

Bembridge is a small town or a large village, very densely populated, and is a very popular place for people from the mainland to retire to. It has good facilities, for example, churches of several denominations, supermarkets and specialist shops, a good village hall with frequent events, a small library, and on the cliff at the edge of Bembridge, there is a Warner Leisure Hotel that used to let the public (including us) in to play bowls and use the swimming pool, although that may have changed now. Outside Bembridge is a small airport, so that stars and the wealthy can fly in for a visit or a stay at their second homes in the lovely Seaview.

The coastal path, in theory, follows the cliffs on the edge of Bembridge, but in reality, muddy footpaths, closed roads and diversions are often in place here.

Whether you have to walk the road, the footpaths or the cliffs, you come out of Bembridge, past the old working windmill which is a great tourist attraction, and onto the cliffs (or beach) of Whitecliff Bay, where a massive holiday park of static caravans dominates the landscape. The paths along the cliff here have always been very muddy, sometimes so bad that they are closed, and on one walk, instead of enduring the cliff path, I coasteered Bembridge Bay and over the rocks onto Whitecliff Bay before climbing back up the cliff after the muddy bits. But be careful of tides if you do that, and be careful of crazy dog walkers and out of control dogs! Every fricking year!

Looming above Whitecliff Bay is one of the landmarks of the Island. Culver Down, with its coastguard cottages and memorial. It is a steep huff and puff up the side of the down for me, and the roaming cattle may get curious and check you out, see if your hair is edible, that kind of thing. Good thing I am used to livestock, unlike some scandalised city folk who were stranded there until I shooed the cattle away one time.

The memorial monument on the down is the Yarborough Monument, the tallest monument on the island, and a guide for shipping, taller than the Tennyson Monument that mirrors it on the chalk down in the west. The monument is dedicated to an admiral who founded the Royal Yacht Squadron in Cowes, Charles Pelham, Earl of Yarborough, who used to pay his crew extra if they signed a contract agreeing to be whipped, if the monument's inscriptions are correct. As far as is known, no member of the crew was ever whipped. I just love to share that story.

The cattle can roam on the road, held back by a cattle grate near the monument, and can cross to the downland the other side of the road, where the old coastguard cottages and a little pub stand. I envy the residents of the cottage, to wake up to those views each day.

The road along the down goes past numerous viewpoints and Bembridge Fort, an old fort that is very rarely open to the public, and then down to the Bembridge road near the airport, and further on it runs along what is known as 'The Downs Road' across the Island's eastern downs.

The Downs Road is scenic, one of the best drives on the Island, with viewpoints looking over Sandown Bay, the Downs, the valley between the downs, and the Solent. There are sometimes ice cream vans and coffee vans up there too, my friend told me the vendors were called 'Stan in the Van' and 'Bill on the Hill'.
There are many trails for walking as well. But the road is a fast one, with reckless driving and many accidents. So be careful.

Back to Culver Down, the down of chalk cliffs and light green grass, jutting out into the sea. When you reach the top of the down, just past the monument, you cross the road and look down over the panorama of Sandown Bay, from where you will arrive at the bottom of the down, Yaverland, along the bay to the huddle of Sandown, the spire of St. Johns and the landmarks of the pier and Napoleon's Landing, and onwards to Lake Cliffs and then Shanklin, and rising above Shanklin, the cliffs of Dunnose Point, and the line of the downs going back inland. It is a magnificent view and I wish I was there now. My favourite thing was to drive down to Yaverland in my spare time and just sit and look over the bay to Dunnose Point.

Culver Down is unfortunately a notorious spot for suicides, that is the bad side of this beautiful sheer down and cliff. The cliffs themselves, as you follow the beautiful remote and steep paths down to Yaverland, change from chalk to the local soft rock and clay known as 'Blue Slip', short for Blue Slipper, an apt name as the cliffs have falls frequently, and the clay is muddy, slippery and unstable. It is advisable to stay well away from the cliff edge. Lower down, the beach of Yaverland stretches temptingly under the cliff, leading to many incidents of misguided cliff climbers getting into difficulties, as well as people getting cut off by the tide. Occasionally sections of the cliff collapse into the sea.

When you arrive at Yaverland, on the outskirts of Sandown, you will walk into a big car park for beach goers, which charges for parking except in the winter. There are some reasonably good eco toilets, and some foot showers for people coming off the beach, there is also a café with seating alongside the sea wall, although they are open short hours and they don't accept credit or debit cards, unless that has changed since I left. Yaverland is on the number 8 bus route, which runs from Ryde to Bembridge, through Sandown and back into Newport. So, after the long lonely trek on the downs, you are back in civilisation when you reach Yaverland.

From Yaverland the round the Island walk follows the promenade down to Sandown, past the zoo, where I once came second in a job interview. The zoo specializes in rescue tigers, so when I lived in Sandown, what is heard hear first thing in the morning is hungry tigers asking for their breakfast. Yes, really! You can hear them all over the town. Next to the zoo is Dinosaur Isle, where the Island rich fossil heritage is proudly shown off, and next to that is a mini golf course, some hotels, and a lovely marsh and lake, although last I heard, that was potentially to be drained and built on. Further down was what locals called the 'Rainbow Park', Sandham Grounds, which used to have a giant slide and a go kart track, but now what remains is the children's playground and a new restaurant.

Sandown Bay from Yaverland to the town is a smooth wide promenade, much like the one between Ryde and Seaview. All the way along is a low wide wall that you can sit on. The road alongside has parking spaces as you come into Sandown, but they are popular, and they cost except in winter. Many people just pull up briefly there, to admire the sea.

When you reach Sandown there are many hotels and cafes. And you may see coaches outside, dropping off and picking up the coach tourists. At the roundabout you will see Victoria Avenue with the bus stops for Ryde. Sandown High Street with its little local shops as well as supermarkets and library, and on your left the road goes back down alongside the sea, where you can hire deckchairs or beach huts from Derek or get a meal in his wife's café, Planet Janet. I recommend them, nice people and decent prices. Good ice cream in the summer. A day in a beach hut in the quiet season (kettle and other conveniences included) and a nice meal at Janet's, is a lovely break from everyday life.

The beach is wide and sandy here, and in the summer, it is packed. The seafront is all big hotels, set downhill from the high street by a very short and steep hill. In my days of delivering the papers round Sandown on my bike, I used to wobble and zoom down this hill to Napoleon's Landing Flats, avoiding the tourists and their coaches, and then huff and puff back up the hill, past the amused tourists.

Up on the crossroads, there used to be a lovely café called Sunnyside Up, but it closed a while back, on that first walk, I had little money and I was muddy from a fall on Culver Down, but when I got to Sunnyside Up, the manager came to the door with a smile, let me in, and was ever so nice as he got my tea and listened to my story of the walk so far. They were always nice at that café, my friend loved it when she came over to the island, we used to have our jacket potato there. I think it was one of their family who rescued me from the attentions of a very drunk man after Midnight Mass one year. The café opposite Sunnyside up does good tea, and there is also one over the road there that is good, and then there is the rock shop. I had to pretend the rock shop wasn't there because I was addicted to their little sticks of soft fruit rock.

Now here is Sandown Pier, quite well known. Like any pier, it is long, goes out to sea, and is full of amusements and slot machines and has a café. It isn't remarkable but it keeps young people occupied in rainy weather.
 There is a postcard by the naughty postcard guy from Ryde, with a picture of a man lying under the pier, looking up ladies' dresses through the slats as they walk on the pier, and saying to his wife 'Your right, the view from here is amazing!'

Now walking onwards towards Shanklin, you pass a food kiosk run by my friend from the homeless outreach, while above is Battery Gardens, with historic clifftop defence buildings. Then you decide to walk the cliffs or stay by the sea on the revetment under the cliffs. Unfortunately, the cliffs have had a number of falls recently, despite being netted to stabilise them, and the path through the cliff top gardens in Lake is now closed so you have to walk round by road to get back onto the cliffs further on. The cliff tops are tranquil, while the sea is far below and you hear the waves breaking quietly. The revetment below is a popular choice, busy with cyclists, dog walkers, runners and walkers. On a high tide with a wind, you really will dodge the waves though, so watch out! A Sandown Man once tried to teach me a counting sequence for dodging waves at high tide. It didn't work for me!
The revetment has various kiosks, as well as toilets (local residents won a battle to keep these open). The cliff top has a café as well.

At the end of the cliffs or the revetment, you come to the promenade at Shanklin. I never took to this promenade, never spent much time down there when I lived just up the road on Atherly Road. I don't know why. There is car parking, which costs. A big toilet block, a children's adventure playground with a pirate theme, and miniature golf. And then there are cafes and kiosks of all kinds, and every flavour of ice cream possible.

Now you have the choice to follow the coast path back up onto the cliffs, perhaps via Shanklin's famous and frankly terrifying cliff lift, or you can walk to the end of the promenade, scramble the beach and past fishing boats and rocks, up the long steep steps to Luccombe.

The view from the top of Luccombe Steps on the cliff path is beautiful, and there are benches there to prove it. This is also the start of an area of big hotels, but within minutes, as you follow the coast path along the quiet Luccombe lane, you are out in the wilderness with the cliffs alongside you.

Past the lovely houses of the hamlet of Luccombe, where I have done some major garden clearances, you go into the woods at Dunnose Point, where a few houses dot the woodland path. There is a lovely retired paramedic up here, who once let me hide on his porch with a cuppa and photo the very tame and acrobatic Red Squirrels that have got to trust him over the years. He owns the land all the way to the cliff top and even the cliff, which, as he says, isn't much use to him.

Now deep into the wood, you climb down paths and steps, descending what is known as 'The Landslip' because that is what it is. Once people would walk down the cliffs here, to the beaches at the bottom, but the slips mean that those beaches are no longer accessible.

At the end of the long climb, you come onto the sea wall at Bonchurch, a remote, quiet and rocky part of the seafront. The houses on the seafront here are nice, second homes, and with warning notices not to trespass. Obviously, tourists round here are curious. This is a lovely and lonely walk most of the time, and as you progress, you will find council displays about the solar system and planets for you to muse on, eccentric but interesting.

The little rocky bays and inlets that you pass come to an end as you approach Ventnor. Look up to your right and see the massive wooded St. Boniface Down, always known to us as Bonchurch Down.

Ventnor is a strange little town, I never took to it, the roads out are steep and can be badly affected by weather, the town is very cut off from the island in a way, and has its own atmosphere. The seafront has a chip shop selling freshly caught fish, while the fishing boats are moored alongside the shop in the little 'Haven' harbour. There is a nice breakwater walk beside the harbour, and there is a scale model of the Isle of Wight, set in a children's paddling pool. Running down to the sea on the steep slope are gardens, well-planted and beautiful, with a waterfall, while green open spaces on the top of the cliff are the ideal place to watch the annual round the island boat race. The town itself has small specialist shops as well as supermarkets, and the churches offer community cafes.

Onwards from Ventnor, you follow the cliffs, walking through beautifully tended open spaces with ponds. This is a beautiful and refreshing cliff walk, down past St. Lawrence and to the rocky Steephill Cove. One of my favourite treats on my walks or when I lived at Ventnor was to stop here for an excellent coffee and a snack, as here in this tiny and remote cove in the cliffs, are several good cafes. Unfortunately, the onwards journey from Steephill on the clockwise coastal walk is a huff and puff uphill back onto the cliffs.

The cliffs now run towards St. Catherine's and the lighthouse, which is set on kind of ledge, where the cliffs now have two levels, the cliffs upwards to the Niton Road with the shelf on which the path runs, and then the cliffs that drop to the sea below the great white lighthouse. You have to climb upwards towards the road after a while, you can't walk through to the lighthouse. Past the village of Niton, you walk out into remote countryside on the road out to Blackgang

On the left are the cliffs, now sheer to the sea, and on the right is St. Catherine's hill, with its tiny historic building known as 'The Pepperpot'.

It is possible to cross the road, walk the hill and visit the Pepperpot. The Pepperpot, also known as St. Catherine's Oratory, is a medieval lighthouse, the only surviving one in Britain. Built by a local Lord of Chale as a punishment for theft when he allegedly plundered a shipwreck. Nearby are the remains of another lighthouse that was never completed, and is known as the 'Salt Cellar'. The views on St. Catherine's Down are amazing.

Blackgang is one of the best-known Island areas, because of Blackgang Chine, the amusement park built in the middle of nowhere and very close to landslips and crumbling cliffs. Above the amusement park, the coast path comes out on a car park, where if you are lucky, you will find a burger van that does tea, homemade cakes, ice cream, and of course, burgers.

The car park edge, often wet and muddy, has plaques, showing you where you are, and distances, as well as telling you that they were arranged by a lone survivor of a massive landslip that took the whole of the road and houses in that area over the cliff, and you can look down and imagine it.

Blackgang Chine has massive car parks, hidden by the cliffs, and the entry fee is steep, so I admit I have never been in, I can hear that it is fun and I have heard a lot about it. It is for children and family, and they do all sorts of theme weeks and illuminations, although in winter it does go quiet.

You walk past Blackgang and down to Chale, either on a muddy footpath, or alongside the main road, with care, as there is no pavement. The view of the sea is amazing, and often you can see the Dorset Coast. I went weak when I first stood looking down the military road cliffs on that first walk, and saw the Dorset coast, because I mistook the chalk cliffs of Dorset for the chalk cliffs of Freshwater, and I thought it would be way too far to walk in a day! You can't really see the Solent gap between Tennyson Down and the Dorset coast.

The Military Road, from Chale to Freshwater Bay, is part of the West Wight, the wild and remote side of the island, and is my favourite part of the Island. The cliffs on the military road used to have numerous access paths and steps down to remote and beautiful beaches, often through the chines, but cliff and chine erosions have closed a lot of accesses, so now if you get down to the beaches, beware of walking too far along the long beaches on an incoming tide, it is possible to get cut off.

Chale is a small but smart village, with a well-tended church, a family run petrol station and garage, a little tea room, a gypsy wagon in a front garden, and a handful of hotels and holiday camps. One hotel has a giant model dinosaur outside, to remind visitors of the wonderful fossils and prehistoric remains found in this area.

The military road part of the walk is a long one, and there is no public transport along here between Chale and Brook, so if you are walking the military road and relying on buses at the end of the day, you had better start early in order to get there before the buses stop, which is afternoon in the winter, and there is only 1 bus per hour. The bus that runs the end of the military road recently won a European award for one of the most scenic routes in Europe, and I totally agree, this area is quite something to see.

Technically the coast path follows the cliff tops along the military road, but severe mud and erosion problems means you are likely to have to walk alongside the road. The original path turns off across Chale recreation ground on the cliff tops, and it is so beautiful there, with the cliffs on your left and the hills on your right, but after the recreation ground and towards the coastguard cottages, the chine, no longer passable, cuts through the footpath and you have to go round it onto the road. Originally the chines were passable, but as they have eroded, only a few can now be crossed, so you will be on and off the road, and it does take energy, and there is mud, except in very dry summer times. But it is the most beautiful remote walk, one of the best. Be careful with the road, it is fast and dangerous.

You will walk and walk here, with just the sea and the sound of surf for company. Eventually you will come up near Brighstone, a lovely village the other side of the road. There are chines here, but also a holiday park and tea rooms that are open in the summer. I used to walk my friend's dog down here as they live in Brighstone, and this is a really prolific fossil area, but keep off the cliffs, they are unstable, as you will see if you cross the holiday park and see where the cliff has eroded right up to some abandoned chalets, and, carefully, look down the cliff and see the chalets that actually went over the cliff in a cliff fall. There is a bath there and other household items that went over in the huts, and they look so forlorn down there.

Now I will share a secret with you, one of my favourite places on earth. Isle of Wight Pearl. Past Brighstone you will approach this on the cliffs. Go to the right of it to walk round to the entrance.

Isle of Wight Pearl is special, it has a lovely atmosphere and an even lovelier café. As you go in, you will think it is too posh to be free to go in, and you will see a lady standing at the reception desk, but it is free, go on in and admire the local pearls and jewellery made from them, you can even fish your own pearl out of water, not that I ever have. The toilets are quite nice, especially on a long walk. But the café is my favourite place.

Some of the café food is a bit pricey, but it is created in an upmarket way, and they don't do jacket potatoes. But they always did a nice pot of tea at a good price, and if I was revising for an exam or it was a special occasion, I would sometimes have a slice of freshly baked cake as well. The staff there remained the same in the time I knew the Pearl, and always recognised me and gave me a friendly greeting. I would sit out on the cliff top benches if the weather allowed, or I would try to get a window seat.
One of my happiest memories there was the Christmas Trees that they hosted as part of the Brighstone Christmas Tree Festival. I never went to the rest of the festival due to being worried about parking, but the Pearl, in the middle of nowhere, with its big car park and loads of space, was my special part of the festival. I would choose my favourite three trees and award them first, second and third prizes in my mind.
The Pearl is only served by the Downs Breezer buses in the summer, it is totally isolated.

Reluctantly moving on from the Pearl, we start the zig zagging and up and down walk onwards towards Brook and Compton Bay. If you look at the hills to the right of the military road here, they look more like Yorkshire Fells than the south of England, and that made my Yorkshire friend very happy. She and her husband had lived on the South Coast for a long time but she still missed Yorkshire, and she loved to visit the Military Road with me.

Eventually you will come to Compton Bay, where there are large car parks, but this is National Trust Land and the car parks are expensive, the surfers often park on the verges by the road. There are good toilets here, washing and changing facilities, and during the day there is usually a food van with ice creams, burgers, and tea.

Compton Bay is one of the most iconic and beautiful spots on the island, it is also the only really good bay for surfing. The area on the cliffs by the bay is very popular for dog walking, while the beach is normally reachable via steep steps, so be careful with your surfboard! Over the years the steps have often suffered due to cliff falls, and been closed, and that could happen at any time. Again, the cliffs here are the soft rock and clay. while further on, in plain view, the hard chalk cliffs of Freshwater Bay and Tennyson Down loom.

All around you at Compton Bay is beautiful. It is a refreshing place to be. But it's time to move on. You cross a stream and follow a winding path. You will be able to see the path for miles. There is a small memorial near the roadside and then the path is on pure chalk, standing out clear against the steep green clifftop slopes. You will come to another memorial with a poignant message. The memorial is to a fifteen-year-old boy who went over the cliff in 1845, the message on the stone is in memory of the boy, who was an only child, but also to warn unwary travellers to keep away from the unstable cliff edge. The sheerness of the cliffs here and the closeness of the path to the cliff and then the fast Military Road is scary. On the other side of the road the down rises steeply and there is a golf course where the down drops down. Now you are approaching Freshwater Bay.

You climb down to Freshwater Bay, it is a unique bay on the island, small and half circular, with white cliffs each side, but a grey sand and shingle beach, and large pillars of rock in the bay. The sea wall runs the length of the bay, and with the prevailing wind and weather coming in through the bay, some of the best waves in bad weather are seen here, smashing against the wall and the cliffs and making a lovely hollow booming sound.

The bay itself has only a few houses and some hotels directly on it, and the lifeboat station. While over the road is a big car park. Parking costs, but you can pay the hotel a pound to park briefly in their car park instead. There is a big block of toilets for those of us caught short on long walks. The road splits and both roads run inwards towards Totland, Alum Bay and Freshwater, with a turnoff to Newport as well. You can visit the local old thatched church here, or the famous Dimbola Museum and Gallery. But the round the island walk now leaves the road and heads up the looming and bleak side of Tennyson Down.

The Walk on Tennyson Down is long and lonely, I have walked it in the pouring rain, an endless silent walk during which I felt like I was walking through a dream that I couldn't wake from. On the down is the statue to Alfred Tennyson, the poet, who spent a great deal of time staying in Freshwater and roaming the downs, finding inspiration for his poetry.

Eventually you reach the Needles Battery, where, as well as old fortifications, there is a row of coastguard cottages. The Needles coastguard station is mainly manned by coastwatch volunteers, including my old friend from church. Keeping shipping and nautical traffic safe off the Needles. The Needles rocks that are one of the island's most iconic and best-known sights.

If the battery and station are closed, it will be hard for you to see the needles stacks, the iconic chalk towers in the sea from there, as the building is in the way of the view. If it is open to visitors it is worth a view and a talk, but if not, walk down to Alum Bay, where there are viewpoints. You may be interested to know that Marconi created the first radio station up here on the Needles Point, and the very first wireless telegram was sent from here.

Alum Bay, the next stop after the tiring walk on the downs, is another landmark island attraction. Out in the middle of nowhere, this theme park and visitor attraction has a lot to offer. There is a chair lift down the cliff to the beach, and the beach has the famous multiple coloured sands that can be bought in bottles. There are fairground rides and shows, the views of the down, the cliff, the sea, the needles, and the New Forest coastline the other side of the Solent. The visitor centre has a glass blowing demonstration, well worth a view, the entry fee for the glass blowing was only a pound when we went a few years ago.

The next part of the journey makes me ponder the Isle of Wight's history, because there, out of place in the island's usual landscape is pure sandy Dorset heathland, just the same as the land directly across the Solent as I walk from Alum Bay to Totland. The walk is relatively brief, moorland with gorse, dark and uncharacteristic of the island.

Totland is a village in the West Wight, very quiet apart from when foghorns on the needles are booming. The phone signal here tends to be bad, which caused me many problems on one year's walk when my friend who was due to collect me couldn't contact me.

After Totland we start to get to the part of the walk that I dread, I do not like Walking between Totland and Cowes, there is nothing endearing for me about most of this section of the walk.

There is a long boring trek through a large holiday park and usually quite a bit of mud. the Solent is the only encouraging view here, and then you walk through Fort Victoria country park, a lesser known island attraction, which has an activity centre for children in the old fort, but I don't know enough about that to say much, I guess school parties go there to learn about nature and the history of the island's fortifications. There are some nice carvings in the wood, trees carved into animal shapes.
As you come out of the country park, you walk alongside marshes, up to the river Yar and its swing bridge over the road into Yarmouth. And there you are, back in civilization.

Yarmouth is a small town, there is very little parking in town but there is a big car park on the edge. The Wightlink ferry port is a major focal point, shipping people and cars to and from Lymington. And through the narrow street from the port, there is a pier, which is a toll pier, used by fishermen. Next to the pier is a café called 'Gossips', my friend didn't like that name but she liked their tea when we went there. The food and tea are good there.
Yarmouth has a castle, a small castle overlooking the pier, run by English heritage, with recreated 16th Century rooms to admire, battlements, and good view of the Solent from its picnic areas, there isn't much else said about it, and I never took the opportunity to visit it.

The small town has a few local and specialist shops and a lovely seascape of the Solent. The town used to hold a major old boat festival, called the Old Gaffers, and I think that they still do, but I think they have cut down on the market side of it where the town closed for stalls and shows. I worked at the Old Gaffers show one year. The beautiful boats are fully dressed out and dressed up, it is all great fun.

The road out of Yarmouth from Shalfleet has beautiful big houses facing the Solent, and due to the views and demand, parking is very restricted along the road there.
The round the island walk goes into the dark and remote Bouldnor Forest. I am scared of forests, and walking that alone was pretty terrifying, especially in the mist, where I used my phone to guide me, but it is a lovely remote spot for hiking, picnics and horse riding.
The forest walk ends near Shalfleet, where the village shop offers a good range of picnic materials if you happen there near lunchtime. There are no public toilets, but I have persuaded the church to grudgingly let me use their toilet before.

Onwards from Shalfleet is a miserable old walk, or it is in my opinion. Through the marshes of Newtown Creek, which is supposed to be beautiful and is famous for wildlife and rare birds. To me it is muddy, the bridges are slippery and treacherous, and it is endless and remote. Onwards to the winding lanes of Newtown, which was once a thriving trade port, but is now a deathly quiet hamlet, with a historic grand village hall. You can walk there for miles and see no one, you could be anywhere in the world.

Out in the middle of nowhere is a cadets and reserve army camp, confusingly known as 'Jersey Camp', possibly to make newcomers think that they are at Jersey Field Squadron in the Channel Islands? But it is good country for exercises.

Now you plunge down into the massive Thorness Bay holiday park just outside Gurnard, originally there was a path on the nearby cliffs, but landslides made it inaccessible, so now you have to walk through the holiday park in order to get down to the sea at Gurnard without dodging crazy drivers on the Porchfield road.

From Gurnard you now have an easy, level and scenic walk alongside the Solent into Cowes. There is a refreshments kiosk halfway, which does a decent tea or coffee. If you look over the road at the exclusive flats there, I used to work on the team that maintained the grounds, so I would take my coffee break here, and there are also useful toilets on the green over the road, open all the time. Gurnard beach is popular with families in the summer, and is also home to local sailing groups and clubs, it is a sheltered beach, facing the Solent and South Coast, with great views of shipping and boats, and during Cowes Week, the seafront at Gurnard is packed with spectators, especially for the fireworks finale. I have been lucky enough to be working down there on Cowes Week and spent my breaks on the sea wall with my coffee, enjoying the races.

A short walk takes you into Cowes, past the entrance to the river Medina and some lovely boat moorings, as well as the new breakwater. As you go into town, you will find cafes, ice cream shops and expensive and exclusive shops, as Cowes is a major port of call for yacht sailors from the UK and round the world. But the best café is called Eegons, and that is where my heart on the wall picture is from, they have hearts all round the walls, where people pay tribute to friends, family and loved ones, and my heart there is for the Isle of Wight, no matter where I go.

The town has a lot of interesting shops, and also expensive ones, there is even a new Marks and Spencer food hall. The fast passenger shuttle to the mainland, the Red Jet, has its terminal here in Cowes, and the town has extensive marinas and boat yards. Cowes is a big town and there are often parking problems as it was never designed for the volume of cars that are now around. The coast path walk goes up the hill through the shopping area, and down to the floating bridge.

The floating bridge, also known as the chain ferry, is now notorious. Once upon a time, the floating bridge ran a smooth shuttle service over the river Medina from Cowes to East Cowes, and it used to be a free service. When the brand-new state of the art floating bridge was towed in, after charges were also brought in for the crossing, it was the end of an era. The era of safe and reliable crossings.

The new bridge had so many faults and caused so many problems, that many people felt unable to rely on the new bridge to get to and from work and school or college. The bridge had mechanical faults, grounded on low tides, damaged cars, caused accidents, and generally people didn't know when the bridge would be in action or out of action. So many people were making the 10-mile trip by road to cross the medina instead of trying to get the bridge or being stumped by an out of action bridge. This has added to the already very bad traffic jams into Newport at peak hours.

I hope they have improved it now, because if you are walking the island on the coast path, you are going to end up with a very long extra journey if the bridge is out of action and if there is no motor launch replacement for passengers. The long way round is a trip into Newport and out the other side, and the congestion can be terrible.

On the other side of the floating bridge is East Cowes, named as one of the best places in the UK to live. Well, it isn't bad. One of the first things you see in East Cowes is the massive Waitrose, the only one on the Island. I used to work on the grounds team for the new housing estates behind the Waitrose so I am grateful to Waitrose for my Waitrose Card and my cups of tea on cold and miserable work days. There is a really bad dental surgery there as well, they really damaged my mouth.

Opposite Waitrose is the Red Funnel car ferry port. I know it well. It means that the area can get congested when ferries arrive and depart.
There are some decent ordinary shops in the area too, and then the residential area stretches up the long hill that you will walk if you walk round the island on the coastal path. At the top of the hill, above the town, you will see Osborne House, the former holiday residence of Queen Victoria and her consort, Prince Albert. The house is now run by the National Trust, and has extensive landscaped grounds, many exhibitions throughout the year, and its own private beach for visitors. I used to know the security coordinator there, he and I went to see the film 'Self/Less' when it came out in the cinema. Nice chap, he used to work in airport security and he had some great stories.

The coast path continues alongside the road out of East Cowes and up to Whippingham. Past the new estates where I lodged briefly with the nicest boys in the world, and there is the ancient Church of St. Mildred's, which was Queen Victoria's Church, and which gets many visitors. The coast path turns onto quiet hedged lanes through the deepest of nowhere, parallel to the main road from Newport to Ryde and down to the residential area of Wootton Bridge, where Wootton Creek crosses the road under a bridge that recently underwent a controversial renovation.

On one side the water is like a lake and has a spa resort beside it, on the other the water is very tidal and full of boats, with a handy pub beside it for thirsty sailors. Wootton is a quiet residential area, loved by residents apart from the smell of the creek, densely populated and with shops and a medical centre. It has one of the best chip shops, which was closed for some time after a big fire, and reopened as good as ever. Behind Wootton, alongside the creek is a very long lane of big exclusive houses, as well as a big holiday camp for disadvantaged children.
Wootton Bridge has one terminal end of the Isle of Wight Steam Railway, one of my favourite island attractions.
Wootton is lucky in having three nice friendly pubs with good food, as well as a part-time volunteer tearoom. There is also a charity shop and several independent shops and enterprises.

Onwards from Wootton you climb the hill, and turn off onto a farm track and down a footpath, and you cross the Fishbourne ferry road, where Wightlink ferries cars and passengers to Portsmouth.
A few minutes' walk and you arrive at Quarr Abbey, one of the Island's attractions.

I used to do some volunteer work for Quarr, on their gardening team, and have also been to Mass there. The Abbey is a working site with Benedictine Monks in residence. The Abbey has tourist and retreat accommodation as well as a grand Church and peaceful pilgrims chapel. There are also tea rooms and an art gallery, a shop, gardens, woodlands, and pigs which people can pay to feed.

The working vegetable gardens and espalier fruit trees add to the memory of when the site was run by the Monks only for sustenance, as now a team of volunteers and paid workers run the site under the direction of the monks, and money raised goes to the upkeep of the abbey and monks. The church has regular masses that the general public can attend, and even local celebrity Alan Tichmarsh has turned up while I have been working there. The tea must be good. I like Alan's books that are set locally in Hampshire and the island. He did a great book called 'Rosie', which made the island come alive for me when I first came to live there.

Onwards from Quarr is the last leg of a round the island clockwise walk on the coast path, and it is a nice gentle walk. My social group would often walk to and from Quarr for a cuppa. The land belonging to the Abbey stretches out towards Ryde through woodland, and there is an ancient wall and some building, I think it's the old Abbey or Monastery, which has recently been restored by heritage builders. There is a quiet exclusive lane. You pass through the edge of Binstead, my old home, there is a small church here with a handy bench and quiet churchyard, then down the lane and onto a path through the golf course.

Let me share a secret with you about this little path, if you promise not to tell. You will come to a stream crossing your path, and a path turns off alongside it. Take the time to go off route and follow the path.
You will come out of the bushes onto a small deserted sandy beach with only a few fishing boats, pots and ropes, and the waters of the Solent will look beautiful in this hidden and deserted paradise. This is Binstead Beach. Amazing isn't it? Don't tell everyone, or it will stop being a hidden paradise.

You head back on the path and to the end of the golf course, and walk down Spencer road with the Solent gleaming ahead of you. And there you are, on Ryde Esplanade. You have seen the changing landscapes of the island and learned a lot about it through my round the island walk on the coast path. So now I will share my experience of life on the island and what is good, interesting, or awful.

Life on the Island.

Ryde.

This was the first town I lived in on the island so I will here.

When mainlanders heard I was from Ryde, they often asked if I knew David Ike, as if a town of 30,000 people was small enough for me to know him personally.

I had seen Ike in Tesco, obviously he has no conspiracy theories about them that put him off buying from them. I knew someone who knew him, a man from volunteering at the homeless outreach, who had been targeted over something and had gained Ike's support. But just because someone lives on the island or in Ryde doesn't mean they know him!

Advertised as 'The town on the Beach', which is a fair description, in Ryde you can see the blend of the town that it was in times past as a seaside resort, and the gritty everyday Ryde now, with its large population and parking issues.

Like most places on the island, Ryde wasn't designed for the level of traffic and cars it now carries, and so congestion and parking problems are rife, especially as there is no scope to change the roads and parking.

Ryde is the largest town on the island but not the capital town, and it climbs the hill from the beach towards Nettlestone and Brading and sprawls out towards Binstead and Haylands, it is mainly residential, with some small industrial areas and a reasonably well-equipped central shopping area as well as a major Tesco Superstore on the edge of town.

The town has a resident-run swimming pool, whereas the rest of the island's swimming baths are run by the council through an organization called 1Leisure.

The beaches are long and Sandy, and there are many cafes and food outlets. It is, in its way, a nice community, but with its share of modern-day problems.

Ryde has great transport links to the mainland and the rest of the island, with passenger ferry and hovercraft terminals, a bus station and three train stations. The pier which hosts the passenger ferry is a very long and very old Victorian Pier, the oldest in the UK, and attracts the interest of many visitors. The train ride along the pier from the ferry to the town is very popular. Ryde also has a nearby car ferry terminal for services to and from the mainland.

There is a tourist information centre opposite the pier, and a local history museum just around the corner and up the hill in the shopping area. The museum showcases the naughty Donald McGill postcards that I mentioned during the walk section of this book, he was a Ryde Artist whose work amused and horrified the tourists of yesteryear. If you are in Ryde Esplanade bus and train station, you can also view some of the postcards there.

Ryde has some great events such as the Annual Scooter Rally, thousands of scooters and riders, dressed up and decorated, gather in Ryde during the August bank holiday for events and ride-outs, it is an amazing sight, they keep the whole island entertained, and slow.

Ryde Pride has been a big event recently, everyone goes, everyone celebrates, and this year (2018) they hosted European Pride, which was a massive event.

Accommodation in Ryde is plentiful and variable. Being a tourist town, there are plenty of hotels near the seafront, there are also bed and breakfasts and caravan parks nearby.

For tourists there isn't a huge amount of entertainment in the evenings, there are some pubs and clubs, a bit of live music, and John staggering down the middle of Union Street, but most go to Newport for evening entertainment.

Ryde has a small independent cinema with limited listings, and there is a bowling alley with refreshments and an amusement arcade, (very nice but the drinks are expensive). There used to be a skate rink, but sadly it closed down, much to the shock and protest of islanders, as the island had skate and ice hockey teams who did really well. When you are on an island and you lose a facility like that, which is the life and joy of competitive youngsters, it can ruin dreams. Some people ferried their children to mainland rinks to complete qualifications and seasons for a while, but it isn't practical.

Ryde's main attraction is the beach for summer visitors, a nice relaxing beach holiday that doesn't cost as much as going abroad.

Ryde has a good speedway track, at Springfield Stadium on the edge of the town. It is well supported by locals. Wightlink Warriors are the speedway team, and in the news now, they are thriving.

Near the street where I lived for a short and miserable time, with dangerous damp and with an antisocial housemate, there is a bus museum. It used to be based in Newport, and moved to the crowded backstreets of Ryde. I never had a chance to visit, but I remember the crowds walking down the road during the now annual bus and beer walks, which involve the old buses carting people round the island to walk to pubs, which is a bit odd and causes a bit of congestion, and a lot of noise at night.

There are wealthy areas and big houses, but it is also a town of very poor accommodation, there are many streets of houses divided into flats, with very little parking and too many cars, and parking is strictly enforced in Ryde as it is in other towns on the island. On the outskirts of Ryde, the housing estates of Haylands and Binstead cover many miles and house many families. This book isn't a glossy brochure, it tells you the realities, and reality is that Ryde is a nice town but not an island paradise. Ryde has several welfare and drop-in centres as well as a foodbank, making sure that the poorest and most vulnerable in the town have somewhere to go for help and food. And there is a jobcentre centrally placed.

My original stay in Ryde was back when I couldn't afford to drive. I was living in a lodging house in Binstead, the only female in a house of men with drink and drug problems. There was no heating, no hot water, no hygiene, there was mould and damp and I developed bad chest infections. But that accommodation was typical of what was available in Ryde, houses with damp, illegal and undeclared tenancies, that kind of thing.

I used to walk into town most days back then, I couldn't afford the bus. I helped in a charity shop, helped at one of the outreach centres, studied in the library, and generally existed while I waited to go back to work. There are many unemployed people in Ryde and the area, it isn't paradise.

I eventually built up to work as a volunteer at Quarr Abbey, testing my health and ability before returning to work. Quarr is too far to walk to and from work twice a week, so I would get the number 9 bus which stopped outside.

Happy memories of Ryde include walks and bike rides to Seaview on the Duver (promenade), and special days when I got to go to the mainland for various reasons. I also enjoying helping with the fellowship of one of the outreaches. That is my Ryde, where I lived and was part of life. The sun is always shining in Ryde in my memory, even though I have seen it in every weather, including the rare snows that the island gets every five years or so.

Sandown.

I lived in several streets close to each other in the main town in Sandown. I also stayed briefly in Lake, which I will write about separately.

Sandown is sprawled in a valley between two lines of hills, to the East the lighter green downs run to culver down and the cliff head at the end of the bay. To the west the much higher and darker downs run to Dunnose Point above Shanklin. The town runs down to the black and gold sand of Sandown Bay, a vast sweep of sand, punctuated by wooden wave breaks that stop the power of the prevailing wind and tide from breaching the sea walls and damaging the town.

Sandown has been a seaside resort all its life, and in the summer the sweep of the bay is thickly populated by sunbathers and swimmers. The pier offers casino style games machines, as well as slot machines. The bay has many cafes and kiosks to choose from, as well as deckchairs and beach huts for hire. And there is water sports equipment hire available, kayaks, dinghies, surfboards etc.

The town is poor, and after the great age of island tourism, when people started routinely going abroad for holidays, Sandown fell into neglect, with major hotel and entertainment sites being left to ruins. Residents became angry as this state of affairs remained for years, and now at last, the derelict sites have been bought and new construction has proceeded, smartening up the town a bit and giving it a new hope.

The town has street after street of Victorian and Edwardian houses, going back from the beach, many are now flats, and the original buildings are dotted with newer small developments where gardens have been sold as building plots. Most of Sandown is fairly poor. The high street has supermarkets as well as tourist trade shops. And there is a part time small library.

There is a railway station at the top of town and bus stops with services to Ryde and Newport in the centre. The other side of the railway there is a rugby club and community centre, along with newer housing estates and a high school that serves the Sandown and Shanklin area.

I lived in Sandown, first in a bedsit in a block that was then condemned by the council, forcing me and the other tenants to leave. I then lived in a house share with an eccentric housemate and a family who were there part time and also eccentric, until they decided to move their friends in, and I left. I then lived briefly in an illegal tenancy where the owner expected me to caretake the place and then moved herself and her family back in with no warning and threw me out. These types of tenancy are typical of the crowded and rather poor streets of Sandown and Ryde.

It is a nice enough town but poor because it was dependent on the tourist trade and nothing could really replace that. Sandown is social, it has cafes, and it has a small amount of live music and a few pub quizzes but not a roaring social scene. There is a small industrial estate. There are churches, mainly small and prim and a bit closed. There isn't really a main community centre, there used to be a youth centre but it closed, and council offices, but they closed to the public. But one thing Sandown does have is a thriving leisure centre with gym and swimming, classes and a café. Unfortunately, the prices have gone up steadily, and doubled since I was a gym member only a few years ago.

During the times I stayed in Sandown I was self-employed, gardening, cleaning, and delivering newspapers round the town and the nearby rural villages of Adgestone and Alvestone as well as delivering takeaways for the local restaurants. I was able to make ends meet and to enjoy the seascape and landscape as well as making use of the local library and leisure centre and studying for a degree in my spare time.

I had a dreadful experience of the local doctors' surgery, who are overstretched and treat patients like objects on a production line, and among many failures, they left me with a broken spine and told me it was all in my head.
I joined in with local activities such as slimming world, running training, church and community events. beach cleans, social activities with my island wide group, and the annual Christmas Eve fun day which closes the high street so that stalls, displays and activities can take place to keep families and children occupied and stress-free as they wait for Christmas.

Sandown is poor but pleasant, it has its share of problems, but it is a community. It is quiet in the winter and crowded and full in the summer. Sandown has no emergency services stations but relies on police and firefighters from nearby Shanklin or Ryde, and ambulances from Newport, which can be an issue when those ambulances try to dash 8 miles for an emergency on sometimes congested and inadequate roads. The town has clifftop gardens and one full size park, known as Los Altos Park, Los Altos means 'The Heights' in Spanish, and the nearby leisure centre and surgery are also known as The Heights, but why the park's name is in Spanish is a mystery.

Shanklin.

I lived in the rather less run-down town of Shanklin for some time. I had an ex-holiday apartment that that was in a block that the landlady was technically illegally letting, as the place was still registered as holiday lets, which tended to cause problems with the post as Royal Mail refused to recognise the apartments as domestic dwellings.

Shanklin has traffic problems like most places on the island, but not as bad as Sandown and Ryde. The town centre has a nice high street with a good range of local shops and chain stores as well as charity shops. There are good public toilets, and there is a library, although it is community run rather than council run and thus on short hours. The town extends up to what is called 'Shanklin Old Village', the real tourist area, where thatched pubs and houses, hotels and tourist gift shops jostle for space and the speed limit is 20mph on the bendy old road where the tourists crowd.
There is also a thriving theatre, upheld by willing locals and volunteers. And a whole district of hotels.

At the back of Shanklin are the beautiful cliffs and beaches, and Shanklin Chine is one of the local tourist attractions. In fact, the island's oldest tourist attraction at 200 years old. The chine is a steep tree-lined natural gorge with a spring-fed waterfall and a history of being used for smuggling. The Chine is lit up at night, and is spectacular. Most tickets to the Chine offer a free return within a week.
I used to know one of the ticket ladies, and she said that sometimes people try to crawl past the booths unnoticed but they get caught. Darn.
The chine has walkways through alongside the magnificent waterfalls, as well as a nature trail, there is a gift shop, and if you go down to the beach, the ancient thatched Fisherman's Cottage restaurant offers food.

While I lived in Shanklin I worked as a freelance gardener and cleaner, as well as delivering takeaways, leaflets and newspapers. I had a reasonable quality of life most of the time. Money was tight but I had food and necessities. Like most of my neighbours, there wasn't much money in our area, but we got by. I never joined in with any community activities in Shanklin. The local churches didn't seem welcoming, so I went to church in Newport or Sandown, and I went back to Sandown for the gym and the awful GP surgery, until I gave up on the NHS and used private online doctors.

I was part of the community as I biked around delivering papers and leaflets, I got to know a lot of people that way. And Shanklin is close enough to Sandown to keep in contact with everyone there. Shanklin was alright, I didn't love it, didn't dislike it, it is pleasant but bland. I didn't go down to the sea in Shanklin much, partly because the hill down to the sea was so steep that to bike or walk it was hard on my asthma, and in the car, the speed bumps down there were off-putting. The views from the cliffs were nice, but made me miss the Channel Islands. Shanklin is well connected, with the bus routes between Newport and Ryde serving it well, and a railway station with trains to Ryde and stations between.

Lake.

I stayed briefly in lake on two occasions. Both times I stayed in badly regulated lodging houses and had a bad time, and didn't stay long. Drug users, drug dealers, fights, poor facilities and dangerous disrepair is the best way to describe it. There was a high turnover of tenants, some people only stayed for weeks.

Lake is part of Sandown, and maybe poorer than Sandown town, there is very little parking and roads are crowded with cars parked at the side of the road. A lot of old hotels and bed and breakfasts have been converted to money-making lodging houses with people crammed in, and some are in poor repair.

Lake has a high street, with a number of takeaways, charity shops, and chemists and others, there used to be a nice co-op but it was driven out of business by a new not so nice Tesco. There is a Lions Club building hidden behind the shops, and sometimes good community and social events are held there, they also run the local beach cleaning parties.

The other side of the road, the railway runs behind the crowded streets, and beyond that is the lovely cliff path and cliff gardens. There is a serious problem with cliff erosion which is affecting the cliff path and leading to closures, and that erosion will eventually affect the roads and houses on that side of Lake. Lake has a small but useful railway station, behind the Methodist church who do a café library and community lunch on alternate weeks.

If you turn onto Newport Road and start heading inland, past the congestion of parked cars, you will see the regeneration of Lake, where a Premier Inn, Restaurant and Aldi have been built alongside the industrial estates, there is also a big Morrisons store there, with a petrol station.

Lake doesn't have any particular attractions or places of interest, although Sandown airport and the holiday park are based there. My time in Lake was about surviving dangerous drink and drug-fuelled antisocial behaviour in the unregulated lodgings houses, while the respective landlords didn't act to control the tenants. But that didn't stop me from enjoying other parts of the island through my sponsored walks and day trips. Lake lets the island down a bit when tourists see it, especially if they haven't seen the West Wight and the full beauty of the island.

Ventnor.

My accommodation in Ventnor was legal and above board, but very basic, as my budget was of course low. The landlord here at least obeyed housing law, but the flats had no sound proofing and were next to a pub. There was no safe parking, and it was a grim street. The landlord wouldn't let me keep my bike at the house, so it had to be left in Shanklin, which meant I couldn't really use it.

Ventnor is a strange town, barricaded behind the down, it is like a different world on its own, especially in bad weather when the steep roads in or out of the town are difficult to navigate.

Ventnor has a microclimate, as it is trapped between the down and the English Channel in its own little space, and that microclimate enables Ventnor Botanical Gardens to thrive in growing tropical and other exotic species of plants. The island as a whole does better with more tender plants than most of the UK, as it is a milder climate.
Ventnor Botanic Gardens used to be a big attraction, even in my early days on the island. But when I offered to volunteer for them, even when they advertised for volunteers, they would never respond. Then the botanical gardens changed hands, changed management, and the high entry fees drove the locals away, there was no discount for locals, and now the botanical gardens attract mainly the coach parties and other tourists. The gardens are situated on a cliffside drive called 'The Undercliff', which has had major problems with landslips and resulting road closures, leading to people avoiding the area.

Ventnor is divided into the main town, and Upper Ventnor, which sprawls up the hill in the direction of Newport, you can also divide Ventnor further by adding Bonchurch, a residential area that runs along the seafront back towards the Luccombe landslip and Luccombe. Just outside Ventnor are the villages of St. Lawrence, Niton and Whitwell.

I lived in the main town in Ventnor, in a street that winds round to the cliff top. Some people would die to live that close to the cliffs and with an oblique view of the sea from their window, but as I often mention of my dear island, it isn't paradise.

The flats I was in were next door to a pub, a pub where drunk people would spend a lot of time outside, talking or shouting, even late at night. There was no off road parking at these shabby old houses by the pub, so I had to either park away in a car park or briefly on the road, with the jeers and stares of the drunk people - although I made a complaint about them at one point as well as telling them in no uncertain terms that as I could actually drive and park and all they could do was drink and make silly comments, they were the losers. That was effective.

The parking outside was for an hour at a time, and the traffic wardens there, as in all the island, were vicious. I never got a ticket, but my landlord often did as he spent a lot of time at the flats, doing repairs and renovations, so much that it was intrusive, in fact, and he lived in Shanklin.

The short and grimy road was like a road from a bygone era, but it had a modern expensive and lacklustre corner shop and the pub, then the road bent round into another road where there was a car park, the town hall, and a police station. The police would often openly stop and see who was hanging around by the pub, which was unnerving, and often a dray lorry would block the narrow road for some time while it unloaded, and as it was a one-way street, residents had no way of getting home and traffic would back up behind the lorry and curses were flung.

The car park round the corner was one that you had to pay for, and I got a permit, which I paid for every six months. That's a major and consistent problem for renters on the island, parking. You will get parking if you are lucky, especially poor renters but even those better off than me as well. I knew a lady who rented a house in Lake, but there was no parking, she would have to park streets away from home and walk back, it's either no parking, risky parking where your car may be damaged, or paid permit parking or even parking that doesn't exist, which experienced at a later property.

So, I had a parking permit for the car park on the cliff top in Ventnor, and I used to park on the edge of the cliff there, literally, the last row of spaces looked out to sea and the land dropped away to the open space and then the cliffs. I parked there not because of the view but because several other local residents who parked sensibly and reliable tended to park there, and I felt that the car was safer from damage there. I hated leaving my car out of sight, I relied on it for my work and also to get out of Ventnor!

The local garden contractors used to strim the area behind the car park and splatter my car, which was annoying. But they were like that, as a gardener myself I was always very careful, but those guys didn't care, they were the same with the local churchyard, there was an enforcement meaning that they had the rights to the contract and they used to drive the church community mad!

My flat was a small, square studio flat with a little kitchen and a small shower room. It was nicely self-contained and small. It was slightly damp, and if I had the windows open, I had to deal with noise from the pub. As well as the rent, there were charges for electricity and laundry facilities. It was a card meter for the electricity, about five pounds a week, and the laundry machines worked on a token basis, that you had to pay for, so in that way it was a good thing that the landlord was always around, otherwise electric cards and laundry tokens would have been scarce.

The landlord wouldn't let me keep my bike at the house, so I had to leave it in Shanklin. But he trusted me with the mailbox key and I would bring in and sort the post for the other residents. There were six flats, all people with low income or health issues, and it got a bit crazy at times, for example one resident brought in a cat when no pets were allowed, and he didn't tell the landlord, the cat had fleas and soon the house did too, someone used a smoke bomb, still not telling the landlord, and it set the fire alarms off. We ended up with two fire engines and loads of delicious firemen around. The pub goers hadn't realised that free entertainment would be on that evening!

Ventnor isn't bad, tourist-wise, Bonchurch Down and the seafront from Bonchurch to Ventnor and cliffs to Steephill Cove are very nice, there is plenty of scenery, and then there's the botanical gardens, where art exhibitions are also held. There's a pub called the Spyglass Inn at the end of the seafront, which is quite well thought of and has a garden with sea views. There is Ventnor Fringe Festival, and not far away is the Donkey Sanctuary. There are pretty parks and gardens, and many hotels. There is also a carnival. And a great attraction to Ventnor every Christmas is the Charity Boxing Day Swim. Hundreds of people in swimming gear or fancy dress, dive in and swim for a Ventnor Charity which enables local people to get to mainland hospitals for treatment without ending up in financial trouble.

I helped with the carnival one year, and it was a disaster, unlike the many others I have helped with.

As a new volunteer to Ventnor Carnival, I was supposed to be briefed on marshalling, but the person briefing had to deal with an emergency, and I was simply given a radio and told where to stand, alone. And unfortunately, the roads people had forgotten to close the road, and the other road was closed due to works, so I got a lot of angry tourists in cars, demanding that I stand aside so that they could drive through the parade as there was no way through and the traffic jam meant no one could turn round.

t is lucky I have done years of marshalling. I didn't give in, I just radioed for help until the chief marshals and road company had to act, and I was opposite the church, where my church friends were doing tea, and they did their best to assist me and bring me tea as well. There were also no clear instructions about returning to base, or where the uncertain fireworks were to go off, if they did go off. I only did that one carnival at Ventnor, and I emailed them and said 'Never again'.

Dear Ventnor, I love to hate it. Out on the Southern tip of the island alone and facing the dark and fierce prevailing sea. Keep the speed down if you drive in Ventnor, the roads are no joke. And here's something about Ventnor that you would expect in the Channel Islands but not here, Ventnor has poor radio signals because of its position, but as you drive the upper roads, the radio sometimes picks up French stations. I liked this when I was studying French, it helped with my comprehension. But more seriously, some say that their phones go onto a French network and they get charged for roaming, again this is more common in the Channel Islands, how the French networks reach the Isle of Wight is incomprehensible. I did wonder if it was the passing Brittany Ferries that caused it.

Newport and Carisbrooke.

I remember being surprised by Newport long before I lived on the island. It was so grim, so run down, with housing estates radiating out from a town centre of grim terraced houses. I wondered how an island that is still known for tourism, could have such a sad capital, and as is the case with many tourists, Newport was one of the first parts of the island I saw, many years ago when I was a teenager. Now one of the first sights tourists get, with the floating bridge so often out of action and simply too much traffic, is the congestion and traffic jams off Coppins Bridge Roundabout and into Newport town centre, out of Cowes or on Fairlee into town.

Newport is smaller than Ryde, although it is growing, with a major new housing development alongside Staplers and down to the Pan Estate, where a new Supermarket has also changed the old landscape. The old streets of Newport are quite dark with the energy saving street lighting, and there are many streets of terraced houses and not enough parking for the volume of residents' cars. There are car parks, and residents can get permits, as I did during my brief stay in the town centre. Car parks aren't cheap in Newport, and traffic wardens are mercenary.

Newport really is a port, of sorts, it is inland slightly from Cowes on the river Medina, but boats and even small barges, can come into Newport, past the very exclusive 'Island Harbour' Marina, a luxury housing complex where everyone has their own moorings, and there is an upmarket restaurant. I used to work sub-contract at Island Harbour, and the residents were very demanding.
Newport Quay is a nice area for walking and cycling, and you can go through there to the playing fields at Seaclose Park, which is famous for the Isle of Wight Festival.
Quay Arts is nearby and offers great work and items from local artists, well worth a visit.

Newport is home to the Isle of Wight Council and the Island's Hospital, St. Marys, which was under special measures last time I was on the island, but I have to say that the staff at casualty can be very helpful even when under pressure.
The town has two prisons for serious and sex offenders, which occasionally worries islanders when trouble breaks out or prisoners are released on the island. The prison estate is dark and very hard to navigate at night if you are a delivery driver, take if from someone who has experienced it. Nearby the prisons is the beautiful but spooky Parkhurst forest, lovely for walks and activities. I used to sit in my car up there and read in the shade in the hot summers.

The town has a cinema complex with the usual handy restaurants and bars. There are plenty of supermarkets, a reasonable library, and a good variety of shops, including independent ones, as well as a ratty bus station. There is even a college nearby, on the industrial and retail estate by the hospital. The college isn't brilliant, especially not for adult education, they get short of students and staff and cancel a lot of courses.

Heading out of Newport on Fairlee, there is a Leisure Centre, which offers swimming, gym, and a variety of classes to suit every level of fitness or ambition. The Leisure Centre is next to the High School, and chaos with traffic is common here as people try to get in and out of the school and Leisure Centre onto the busy Fairlee Road.

Newport's Central Church is the Minster, well known for dignitaries and ceremonies but with little architectural interest, that kind of thing. The rest of us go to the little evangelical churches hidden nearby. There is a nice chip shop near the minster though. And dotted round and about are hidden gems of shops, book shops, a scoop and weigh, and a shop selling specialist teas, among others. Newport has a small community theatre called the Medina Theatre, and also a reserve forces squadron based at Drill Hall Road.

Hidden among the back streets of Newport, where the houses are crowded and there is no parking, there is an unexpected attraction, Newport Roman Villa. It was discovered accidentally by a home owner doing some work on their property, and is the remains of an ancient dairy farm.

Heading out of Newport to the south is a cycle track that takes you through beautiful peaceful countryside to Sandown, it's an 8-mile ride on smooth even track, which is an old railway line. You even bike through the old station platforms at one point. There used to be a café at the old station when I used to bike through, it's probably still there.

Coming into Newport from Ryde on Staplers are a few hidden gems for visitors, which the locals tend to hear about if there is an accident or closure on Fairlee or Staplers...'Traffic is backing up to Isle of Wight Lavender, Monkey Haven, Butterfly World'. These three attractions, close together, are worth visiting in one hit, if you have the money.

Monkey World, which rescues primates of all kinds, as well as Owls and other creatures, was a story of gritty determination and triumph by a family who came to live on the island and set up the sanctuary. It took them great effort and persistence to make it a success, an inspirational story, and it is now a thriving, award-winning and very worthwhile attraction. There is a souvenir shop and opportunities for Birthday parties or to be keeper for the day.

Butterfly world, has hundreds of butterflies flying free in a natural environment under cover, as well as Japanese and Italian gardens, fountain world fountain displays, and an extensive garden centre as well as a coffee shop, as well as Koi fish ponds, (but shh, it's owned by a man in Dorset, not an islander).

Isle of Wight Lavender has The Old Dairy Tearooms, where you can even experience lavender ice cream. You can view the lavender crops and also see them being distilled in the summer. There is a shop where you can purchase lavender cosmetics and toiletries.

Heading out of town the other side, to Carisbrooke, the first terraces of houses on Carisbrooke Road look smart as well as old, and are mainly divided into flats. I once stayed briefly in a room in one, the rent was huge and the landlady was simply running it as a get rich quick scheme for herself, the house needed repairs all the time, but didn't always get those repairs, and the turnover of tenants was massive. This was the one with the phantom parking, hence me getting a permit, the landlady let the room to me with a promise of a parking space, which turned out not to exist, so I had to park 10 minutes away in a public car park.

Carisbrooke is again a nightmare for traffic and parking, it's a real game of dodging other cars at times, but it has redeeming features, including driving through fords if you go onto the little lanes, which is nice in summer, but imagine me in winter, needing to get to a delivery the other side of the ford and being afraid of being washed away! The other features of Carisbrooke are the old Priory,
which is open as a centre for peace and healing, especially for those seeking peace of mind. There are worship services and retreats held there, and the house and gardens are open daily.

Nearby is one of the Island's biggest attractions, Carisbrooke Castle. The castle was built in anticipation of the Spanish Armada invading, and became the home to one of Queen Victoria's family when she was high sheriff of the Island. Other Lords and Sheriffs also stayed here, as well as King Charles 1 while he awaited execution. His death warrant is displayed at the chapel up there, of all places. I spent a day at the castle, doing a photo shoot and write-up, and I would recommend it to anyone. The staff are nice, the walk along the walls is incredible, and the museums and gardens are fascinating. There are also donkeys, who are trained to work the water wheel and bring fresh water up from the well.

I lodged with an eccentric old man in Carisbrooke, just for a few months. The parking situation left my car a bit battered, and there was nothing really nice about living in that area, but at least it was on the edge of fields and hills and handy for biking the lanes and fords to the castle, it was also handy for the quickest road through to Shorwell and Brighstone to see my friends and take their dogs for walks on the Military Road cliffs.

One of the things I liked about Newport, for all its parking and congestion problems, was that at night, those grim dark streets have a special magic. There isn't a whole lot of violence in Newport on weekend nights, there is more in Ryde, and Newport in the dark is kind of special, and in the early morning too. McDonalds opens at 5am, and the town is small enough to be quiet at that time of morning, it is pleasant then. I did delivery driving work round Newport in the evenings, so I knew the dark roads very well. I did various gardening jobs around the town as a freelance gardener, and as with living there, finding parking in order to work was very difficult.

A bit about other towns and villages, which I haven't actually lived in but will have mentioned in my walk chapter of the book. There are other little villages, Hamlets and oddments knocking around, but they are just a few houses in the lovely island countryside so I will focus on the bigger areas.

Freshwater and Totland.

Freshwater and Totland sweep the corner of the West Wight, almost blending together, they share the quietest and most remote corner of the island, with the Western Yar river for company. Freshwater has a very old and special thatched church. The town also boasts a special museum and gallery, the Dimbola museum and Gallery, run by a trust dedicated to the name of Julia Margaret Cameron, a famous Victorian photographer who lived and worked here.

Freshwater is also the old home of the poet, Alfred, Lord Tennyson, who would wander out onto the downs for long periods, drawing inspiration for his work. The seascape and landscape around this area is beautiful, with the downs, Freshwater Bay, Totland Bay and Alum Bay and the cliffs in between the bays. There are many walks through this beautiful scenery, and at Alum Bay there is the Amusement Park and chairlifts down the cliff to see the famous multi-coloured sands. My favourite attraction is the glass-blowing demonstration in the visitor centre.

Yarmouth.

Yarmouth is a small town and with old streets and numerous pubs, also home to the Wightlink Ferry connection with Lymington. It is a big sailing town, with a lifting road bridge that enables boats to move to and from the river Yar and moorings.

There is extensive marshland on the western side of town, beside the river. One of Yarmouth's big attractions for more mature tourists is the Grange, a Warner Leisure Hotel and Spa designed for more mature people, no children allowed.
Further west towards Totland is Fort Victoria Country Park and learning centre, designed to get children interested in nature and history and incorporating a marine aquarium in the old fort. There are woodland hikes and trails, and looking out to see from the Country Park, you see Hurst Castle the other side of the Solent but seeming so close on its own spit of sand.

Yarmouth Pier is a toll pier, you have to pay to go on the pier and get that exclusive view of the Solent and mainland, but the view is pretty nice from the shore, the island coastline and the close mainland New Forest Coastland. Parking for Yarmouth is mainly in a big car park on the edge of town, by the river, and the buses for Newport, Freshwater and Totland stop close to the ferry port.

Going East out of Yarmouth, you can go inland to the 'Middle Road' as it is known, the fast road through the downs, which has many accidents unfortunately. Or you can remain close to the coast and go towards Shalfleet. The houses on the east side of Yarmouth are quite big, and those with Solent views are probably worth a pretty penny. As you leave Yarmouth, the dark and remote Bouldnor forest comes between the road and the sea. The forest is nice for hikes and rides and as you follow the forest trail, you get an exclusive view of the Solent from there.

Shalfleet and Calbourn.

Shalfleet is the town on the outside road. Between Yarmouth and Shalfleet is West Wight Alpacas, who normally have tea rooms, although last I heard, the tea rooms had to close temporarily.
Alpacas are lovely chatty sociable animals who, when well-handled, are a delight to spend time with, they are full of life and mischief. I believe that the Alpaca farm has opportunities for walking with the animals and handling them. I am lucky to have worked with alpacas elsewhere and I would say that this would be a special place to visit.

Shalfleet itself is a rural village. They have a well-stocked shop and a reputedly very good pub. And a very annoying set of traffic lights where the road becomes one way just past the church. Apart from that, it really is just a quiet village. There are bed and breakfasts there if you are keen on the countryside and maybe exploring Newtown Creek, and there used to be a tea rooms by the car sales lot on the edge of the village, but I am not sure if it is still there.

Calbourn is the village on the middle road, parallel to Shalfleet. Calbourn has a pub called the Sun Inn, which does roast dinners to die for, I can assure you. And Cabourn also has a historic working water mill and activity centre, well worth a visit. As with Shalfleet, it is a quiet village, but beautiful with the downs behind it, and very well kept.

Chessel Pottery is just outside Calbourn on the way to Freshwater, and offers pottery displays and sales, as well as an excellent tearoom with a very good reputation.

Cowes, Gurnard, Newtown and Porchfield.

Cowes is a world-famous town, not a big town nor a remarkable one in most ways, it is famous for Cowes Week, the international sailing regatta. Cowes week was one of those great nuisances that we would have to put up with, the traffic and parking in Cowes and on the island in general during Cowes week was a nightmare! Imagine trying to work in Cowes if you were a gardening team with a van, a car and sometimes a truck as well, to find parking for.

The moorings and marinas for boats at Cowes are extensive, and extend up the river to Island Harbour, with moorings on the river, on pontoons and also a lot of dry boat parks. The mouth of the Medina now boasts a brand-new breakwater, which the Wight Smiles artist captured perfectly in his cartoon of boats bashing into the breakwater while their helms swore. The breakwater is a long concrete structure, which will never look quite as if it belongs, but I guess it has a purpose. The views from Cowes are of the Medina and Solent, and you can watch boats, ferries and ships daily, the water is never without some marine traffic to watch.

The town is smart and has upmarket and boutique shops, due to the high levels of visiting sailors, not just during Cowes Week but all year round. There are cafes of all kinds, but my favourite, where my little paper heart sits on the wall, is Eegons, who do excellent food as well as the best coffee on the island. They have a great sense of humour and community, and the walls are full of jokes and local articles. I recommend them to you. Say hi to them from me...and they will say, 'WHO?'

There are also various museums around town, including a maritime museum, inevitably. And if you want to get into sailing, there are boat estate agents as well as vendors of boat berths. And there are plenty of sailing clubs and groups to join.

Cowes is home to the infamous floating bridge or chain ferry, sometimes known as 'Floaty McFloatface'. Once upon a time it was a reliable and free way to cross the Medina, a crossing of about two minutes. But there's nothing like modernization to wreck a perfectly good thing, and fees were introduced for the traditionally free crossing, and a new floating bridge was brought in, which has spent its time in service breaking down, damaging cars, causing accidents and being useless and out of action on the biggest spring tides. Last I heard, they were having to use a barge to bolster it.

Cowes Stretches back towards Newport, row upon row of houses, and further back, some have a small driveway, which eases parking problems, apart from where people park across the driveways! It is nice to look back on the island's parking problems and smile, but it wasn't fun to live with those problems! On the edge of Cowes is Northwood, where the County Showground hosts the island's yearly agricultural show. Next door to the showground is the less well known and relatively new Military Museum, well worth a look. I have been there a few times but without time to view the museum at leisure as I was at meetings with volunteer groups who met there. I regret not taking the time, as I find military history and all history fascinating. There are whole tanks there among other features. There is a 1940s café there, I can't remember the name, but as long as tea and cake existed back then, I am sure it's good.

A short walk along the seafront from Cowes is Gurnard, a lovely area with many holiday homes and large houses, some of which I gardened for. The seafront is a long and lovely stretch of sand and shingle beach, very popular with visitors. The beach has a direct view across the Solent to Southampton Water, Bramble Bank (famous both for the grounding of the Houge Osaka and the low tide cricket matches played there on the tidal spit), as well as the long rows of beach huts on the corner of Southampton Water and the New Forest coastline. My old friends from Southampton always told me that they waved to me across the water from their beach hut.

Gurnard has a nice refreshment kiosk and nice public toilets, and further up it has a nice café, lifesavers when we worked down there in the freezing cold. There are sun shelters and benches and a lovely even walk alongside the sea for a mile or two. The seafront here also hosts several sailing clubs.
In bad weather and on big tides, the sea can come over the wall and flood the road.
Further up are more holiday homes and the road turns inland, where new housing estates are being built, I have worked on the grounds of these as well. Gurnard Pines is a very large holiday park, and there is also another huge holiday park towards Porchfield but stretching down to the sea, known as Thorness Bay Holiday Park. It's one of many parks where delivery drivers have to phone clients and ask them to come to reception as it is usual to get lost trying to find a particular cabin on the park.

Porchfield is a small and very rural village. I used to caretake a smallholding there. It was lovely at night, total silence apart from the distant sea and the animals, and the skies were beautifully dark. Porchfield has a pub and bed and breakfasts around, including farm bed and breakfasts. The smallholding I worked for had accommodation to let. There isn't much by way of attractions directly in or around the village, but it is close to Cowes and Gurnard, Newport, Carisbrooke and Newtown.

Newtown is a small and even quieter village. It is hard to believe that it was once a major and thriving port for the island. Now it is lost in dreams, down small and quiet lanes in the countryside. I have walked through there without seeing a soul, but it is beautiful in the spring with the daffodils in bloom. Newtown has two things that are mentioned to tourists, one is the old and grand town hall, which is said to show what this sleepy village used to be, the thriving port. But to me, the town hall seemed small and forgotten. Closed and with no one there. Nearby Newtown Creek is the other attraction. Run by the National Trust, the area is a major wildlife and birdlife area, but there is also scope for kayaking, and boats can sail in to a certain point and even moor on the creek. To me the creek was hard work on my walks, round the winding and muddy paths and along the treacherous wooden bridges, don't walk it alone, it is so easy to slip.

East Cowes and Whippingham.

East Cowes, the opposite side of the Medina from Cowes, is the cheerful side of town, or is it? The parking can be a nightmare. And don't call East Cowes part of Cowes in front of the locals, they may lynch you. Don't say 'West Cowes' and 'East Cowes' either, trust me on that.

If you look over the river from Cowes, you will see the great boat building yards of East Cowes, still proudly in operation. The newest Red Jet fast passenger ferry was built here. You will also see, further up the river, the ancient iron crane, a Grade II listed protected feature that is from the bygone days of great ship building days here, it came into service in 1912, when the ship building industry on the island was bigger, and is now no longer in use. There is also a boat museum here, not far from the ship building yards.

I never had an opportunity to visit the boat museum, which is a shame as elsewhere I have loved visiting boat and maritime museums, my enthusiasm for boats and all things maritime is as great as it was in my award-winning sailing days. I guess I was never in East Cowes and not busy. Along the beautiful promenade from the boat museum, past the children's paddling pool and play area, there is a castle. Although at time of writing, landslips are making navigation of the seafront difficult, so beware. The castle is Norris Castle.

Set on a hillside, and now growing rapidly with a massive new housing estate down by the ferry port and a fair-sized new housing estate alongside the river and up into Whippingham further along, East Cowes came into the top five places to live in the UK not long ago. And it isn't bad. The over 100-year-old Umbrella Tree outside the town hall is apparently one reason that East Cowes is loved, as well as the Waitrose. The Umbrella Tree has been a subject of fierce debate recently, it is old, it is a feature and fixture, and it has been diseased, so the council wanted to chop it down. The locals have been fierce and there have been fights about it. The striking tree is reputed to have been planted by Queen Victoria's head gardener and also has a circular bench around it.

I worked on the former gardening team on the lower new estates of East Cowes and also lodged in a house on the upper new estate for six weeks before I left the island to continue my travels. It's an OK place, it has one main problem. If the floating bridge is out of action, as it frequently is, and there is an accident on the main road, the only route out of East Cowes if you can't get onto the back lanes, then you are stuck, and as it is a fast road and with hourly waves of traffic heading to and from the car ferry and high volumes of traffic. If an accident closes the road, you can be totally stuck, for hours.

On a happier note, East Cowes has a good choice of supermarkets, including Waitrose, as well as a library, local independent shops, nice views, a lovely promenade, and am I forgetting something? Oh yes, it used to be the second home of Queen Victoria and Prince Albert. And Osbourne House and Albert Cottage are still there, attracting high volumes of tourists to view the regal landmark house and museum, the beautifully kept grounds, the trails, the private beach, and the numerous exhibitions. Well worth a visit.

GKN Aerospace has works at East Cowes, on the site of the old Hovercraft factory which it developed from.

Whippingham, the village just up the main road out of East Cowes, has a special church, St. Mildred's Church, which was once Queen Victoria's church when she was on the island, and Prince Albert was involved in the design of the church. There are Royal Tombs within the church, as well as plaques dedicated to members of the Royal Family and several Royal and notable graves in the churchyard.

Tours of the church are available, and there is also a nice chatty lady vicar, who will be very happy to see you and answer any questions, if she has time. There is plenty of parking and I think there is some form of visitor information available at the adjacent church hall. I used to walk my friend's dog up there in the evenings in the heat of summer, so I never went in the hall and visitor information area, indeed never went in the church, which is my loss.

Shorwell and Brighstone.

Heading back inland now and towards the villages that dot the centre of the island. My favourites, Shorwell and Brighstone are towards the Military Road, the straight old road that runs from Chale to Freshwater Bay, and which is in serious danger due to cliff and chine erosions which destabilise the road. Shorwell is considered to be part of Newport by some satnavs and maps, even though it is a few miles out. Shorwell is a sleepy and quiet village, there isn't much to see except lovely countryside and downs walks, and also parts of the old railway line that long ago ran through the area. There have recently been extensive works to stabilise a historic viaduct there.

Brighstone, the next village, (don't tell me Limerstone is a village!) is a bigger village and closer to the cliffs and holiday parks as well as having great access to the downs. Brighstone is known for its annual Christmas Tree festival, with hundreds of trees supplied and decorated by individuals, charities, groups and organizations. It is a big event, which uses various venues including the church, pub and the nearby Isle of Wight Pearl's café area. Grange farm at Brighstone has an extensive holiday park with a chineside track down to the sea alongside the rushing waters of the stream that falls down the chine.

There is an extensive stretch of golden beach, sheltered by the cliffs, and miles of cliff-top walks. I used to go to Brighstone to my friends, who made the best homemade scones, cakes and flapjacks, I used to walk their dog on the cliffs or beach, and go back to have hot tea and homemade baked goodies, and I always thought that this was what paradise must be like.

Brighstone also has a small local museum, and outside Brighstone is Mottistone Manor, owned by the National Trust, a Grade II listed manor with stunning and very popular landscaped gardens. The house isn't open to the public, but the gardens are, and there are tearooms. The house dates back to the fifteenth or sixteenth Century and was the family home of the Seely Family, who the current local MP is related to. The wedding of Benedict Cumberbatch and Sophie Hunter was held here, but islanders didn't know about it until they saw them leaving the site.

Whitwell, St, Lawrence, Niton and Chale.

The villages between Ventnor and the Military Road are scenic and quiet and set in lovely countryside. That countryside contains some of the most eccentric people around, but you never mind that, I will write about it in 'The confessions of a gardener'.

The quiet village of St. Lawrence suffers the constant headache of landslips and erosion closing the roads. Hidden below the village is the beautiful gem of Steephill Cove, where several nice cafes offer refreshments with full views of the beach, the rocks, the cliffs, and the English Channel. Further along the cliffs, on that curious ledge between upper and lower cliffs, St. Catherine's Lighthouse keeps shipping safe from the rocks at St. Catherine's Point.
Further along the road from St. Lawrence, Whitwell is a very small village, the road goes through the village, which has a church and a petrol station, as well as a hidden park farm with holiday lets, fishing lakes, and attractions for visitors, including reindeer.

The turning for Niton is by the church in Whitwell, and the distance between the villages is about a mile. Niton has a grocery store and a one-way system that baffles the tourists. It doesn't have a whole lot else. But when you drive out the other side of Niton, you come to the most glorious landscape, St Catherine's Down sweeps up on one side of you, while the English

Channel over the cliffs is dazzling. There are accidents here as it is a beautiful view, a fast road, and popular with bikers as well. Towards the end of the road, a car park in the cliffs offers beautiful views, a place to park and take a walk in the stunning landscape, and during the daytime apart from deep winter and bad weather, a food van.

Down the hill the famous Blackgang Chine and its amusement park is hidden, and by all accounts well worth a visit.
just beyond that is the small village of Chale, with a church, petrol station, tea rooms and holiday accommodation. Chale is at the start of the military road cliffs, and the recreation ground on the cliff top hosts the biggest horticultural show in the island once a year, as well as vast car boot sales on bank holidays, and also acts as a starting point for charity hiking, running and biking events. There are some extremely handy portable toilets permanently there, very handy, let me assure you.

Wroxall, Godshill and Rookley.

Wroxall is the nightmare traffic bit just as you go out of Upper Ventnor, but although it is classified as a village, it seems like an extension of Upper Ventnor. There are cars parked along the road and cars and buses weaving in and out and trying to shoot through the parked cars hazards before cars from the other direction get in the way, another delight of the Isle of Wight. There are several pubs and shops in Wroxall, and technically the Donkey Sanctuary is under the Wroxall boundary. There is also another attraction, well-hidden and sometimes overlooked. Appuldurcombe House.

Appuldurcombe House was once a grand stately home, home of the Worsley family. The house still stands but is unoccupied, and during the week is open to visitors for free. There are also self-catering holiday homes located in the extensive grounds. The gardens were designed and landscaped by Capability Brown, the famous landscape architect. At weekends the house is closed to visitors and operates as a licenced wedding and reception venue. The site used to have a falconry centre, but that may have closed. I think it merged with the one at Havenstreet.

The villages of Godshill and Rookley are set inland from Ventnor, on the road to Newport. Nice villages, busier than those described so far, and on the main road. Behind the villages the downs still tower and keep the scene green as the traffic hurries through.

Godshill is a major tourism village, designed for tourists and very similar to Shanklin's old village with the thatched roofs and the gift shops. The pride of this small tourist village is the perfect and extensive 'model village' which has exactly replicated the village itself, they also have a model of Shanklin Chine.
There are cafes and tea rooms, there are pubs with nice gardens, there are gifts shops. And there are also tourists all over the road. Some of the village has no footway, and so people walk on the road. The speed limit is 20mph through the main village, but impatient drivers, hazardously parked buses and people suddenly jumping onto the road, makes it treacherous, especially as not all drivers respect the speed limit.

Hidden to the sides of the village are extensive car parks, including coach parking spaces for the coach tourists, which are many. The island's roads get jammed with slow coaches, which is no joke, especially not for a busy freelancer, hurrying between jobs. Also slightly hidden is the medieval church on the hill. One of the local pubs does a sausage and cider festival in the summer. Sausages, cider, entertainment and stalls. I can vouch for the sausages, the entertainment and the stalls, but I never tried the cider. The non-alcoholic Coca-Cola was alright.

Rookley has a country park and extensive caravan park, although the future of the caravan park is uncertain since it was taken over the other year, and residents were apparently given notice. Off the main road there are some nice houses and cottages, including the ancient thatched Holly Cottage, which goes back centuries and holds the secrets of a lot of Rookley's history through the family who lived there, held a church there, and who still own it through a god daughter of the family. The garden was hard work as I was only allowed to do one day a month there. Behind Rookley is the wonderful vista of Bleak Down, the stark and aptly named towering hill that is one of the views that makes the island beautiful.

Havenstreet.

Wonderfully out in the sticks and in the middle of nowhere, Havenstreet is closest to Wootton and Ryde, and easily accessible from the main road between Newport and Arreton. It could be called a hamlet, but it is mainly quite big properties with land along with newer social housing. Havenstreet has several good pubs, great roast dinners. It also has a church. But let me share that secret with you, its big attraction is the Isle of Wight Steam Railway. Havenstreet has the main station.

Havenstreet Station has lots to see, old trains and coaches, extensive museums including a large building called 'Train Story' which tells the story of the Isle of Wight Steam Railway, including the branches that no longer run. The story is told through videos, interactive areas, wall posters and full-size old trains and platforms that you can walk onto and see how things were historically. It is all a lovely experience, as is riding the trains, unmissable if you are on the island. Rodger works there, so say 'Hello Rodger' when you see him.
I spent a day at the steam railway one time, doing photography and a write-up, but that would be too much to include here.
Havenstreet Station has another attraction, separate but working with the station for the sake of visitors. The Falconry Centre. There is an arena for falconry displays, and they are awesome! The birds are well trained and bonded with their handlers, the shows are amusing as well as amazing, and the birds trot round the benches and say hello in between acts. The centre itself is open for visitors, and you can volunteer there, well, you can volunteer if you can get the staff to communicate with you about volunteering. I tried to arrange to volunteer once, and in the end, I gave up and took something else on. But the falconry displays are unmissable.

Havenstreet is a sleepy and peaceful place with lovely gardens and houses, the only problem I remember with the area is flooding in bad weather, the road could flood in the winter, although they may have done work to prevent that now. The only other problem was getting stuck behind a coach when I was in a hurry to get to work. If the road through Wootton is closed for any reason, traffic tries to go through Havenstreet, and it isn't designed for heavy traffic.

Arreton, Branstone Cross, Newchurch, Winford and Apse Heath.

In the Centre of the Island is Arreton with Branston Cross, Newchurch, Winford and Apse Heath. Arreton is a reasonable sized village on the main road, while the others are smaller areas, Branstone Cross is hardly known, just the few houses in the area of the dangerous cross roads towards the top of the main road known as Arreton Road, but I know it because my late friend lived there.

Arreton is a prominent village on the main Newport to Sandown Road, the big fast road known as Arreton Road. The village is strung along the sides of the main road, with a post office and school, and a lot of houses that have names not numbers, and thus are hard to find if you are delivery driving! There have been a number of accidents in the village despite the enforced speed restrictions, including a lorry going through the wall of a house and narrowly missing the elderly occupants who were in bed. Red faces for the local lorry firm, but I think the couple were afraid to return when the house was repaired.

On the Newport side of Arreton is a major road junction which causes major headaches, as there is a fast bend from the Newport direction, a lot of uncertain drivers from the Arreton Direction, and a lot of impatient drivers from the turning towards the Downs Road. It is typical of Isle of Wight traffic problem. But on the corner of this junction is quite a well-known complex called 'Arreton Barns'.

Arreton Barns is a specialist crafts and handmade goods complex, with little booth shops and stalls. Very nice and well worth a look round. There are also displays and exhibitions, including glass blowing, and there is a well-known pub called 'The Dairyman's Daughter', which serves food, a friend of mine doesn't recommend the food but I have never been there. There is a children's play area as well. The barns get busy during tourist season and coming up to Christmas, so there is a (muddy) overspill car park, which is a field.

Arreton and the neighbouring areas have their share of interesting places. Further along at the Bathingbourne crossroads to Newchurch, there are multiple interests. One is the Garlic Farm, which is open to the public and has tea rooms and once a year holds a big festival called the Garlic Festival, with live entertainment, stalls and attractions. Wonderful, and as with all big attractions on the island, it clogs the area up with traffic.

Alongside the main road there is a massive tomato production unit, which sends tomatoes and other salad products all over the UK and even the world. I did a day's work experience there and found it very difficult. It is like working in a factory, but a very hot one, and I was the only English worker there among the hardworking migrant workers. The shifts are 7 till 2 and 2 till 7, and so you see the migrant workers biking and walking miles from the neighbouring towns for their shifts, as buses are only once an hour and don't match up with the shift times.

But if you turn off to Newchurch, Winford and Apse Heath, you can visit Thompson's garden centre with their massive array of plants, and have a meal or a pot of tea in their very nice café. The café cat may come and say hello to you as it wanders round the garden centre. The toilets are very plush. and the café has WIFI. Further up the road you can visit a few more humble family-run plant nurseries, which are also very nice.

Next to Thompsons is another big island attraction, Amazon World. This was originally a family enterprise, and it took off and grew, becoming award-winning and famous, probably because it is wonderfully interactive and has many unusual species. Amazon world has large aviaries of exotic birds flying free, and you can walk through them. The birds can fly over you and poop on your head. Now you won't see that written in a conventional guidebook!

The other side of the aviaries you come out into the main animal areas, where you can see all kinds of exotic species such as red pandas, Lemurs, Capybaras, Ocelots, Anteaters, Meerkats, and much more. You can also meet the Wallabies and feed them, they are curious and sociable. There are play and picnic areas and a gift shop and café. I volunteered briefly for Amazon World but I became too busy with work. My volunteering consisted mainly of a lot of poo picking in the Wallaby enclosure and a lot of poo clearing in the aviaries. I get all the poo jobs in life.

Thankfully Thompsons and Amazon World share a large car park, so you should be alright for parking here! There are often coaches parked, but there is plenty of room. My late friend from up at Branstone Cross said she remembered the island before the coaches were all year round, as they are now. You can get stuck behind a coach when you hurry for the ferry at any time of year now!

Round the corner and less well-known, is the Isle of Wight's Observatory. Now this is a gem. They do open evenings, it used to be on Thursday nights. If you can get there for an open evening then do. I think they do refreshments and it is very sociable and nice. You can watch a slide show or listen to a talk about astronomy, and best of all, you can get a look through their telescopes, with a knowledgeable instructor guiding you. If you get a clear night, what you can see of stars and planets is amazing. I hope that you will find it as fascinating as I did. You can also learn from the observatory about 'Dark Wight Skies', a project to minimise light pollution on the island to make astronomy better as well as encourage wildlife.

Up the road to Branstone Cross, there is another independent plant nursery, a very nice one but no café. And there is a woodland and natural burial ground, Springfield, where each grave has a tree planted on. There is a nearby café and a dangerous stretch of road where many accidents happen, so be careful. When accidents happen at the crossroads up here, the Arreton Road is often closed and traffic chaos occurs. Now you won't find that in the guidebook.

Back to the other side of Arreton, finally, on the edge of Newport, is Robin Hill Country Park, where various events are held through the year, and activities are available. There is adventure play, rides, falconry and more. One of the big attractions is 'Electric Woods', where the park is illuminated in recognition of Diwali the festival of light, and 'A Taste of the Orient' in honour of the Chinese New Year. You can walk through the woodlands with the trees all lit up. It is a cheerful attraction to visit as the nights get darker and longer. The only thing you have to be careful of is traffic, turning off on that treacherous roundabout, as no drivers ever expect anyone to go to Robin Hill. And you get queues of traffic from that roundabout to the local refuse tip too.

On the Newport side of Arreton is a slightly controversial, muddy and smelly operation, a biofuel plant. This opened while I lived on the island, and the road around it became muddy with tractors and trucks bringing crops to be converted to biofuel. It smells, it creates biofuel, but there is another side to this new plant that not everyone knows.

We had an apprentice on the gardening team who gloomily told us about it. He had a smallholding, and the farmers who normally sold him feed crops for his animals on the smallholding were now sending the feed crops to the biofuel plant as they earned more that way, and buying animal feed in was costing too much, as it had to be brought in from the mainland, so this apprentice of ours was having to sell his smallholding, hence joining us as a gardener. A lot of small farms on the island have gone out of business due to costs, not just because of the biofuel plant though. In my last year on the island I remember one of the established old dairies selling up.

Seaview, Nettlestone and St. Helens

Now we fly from the centre of the island to the villages in the Eastern corner.
I have already mentioned these areas in my walk, but they deserve a quick ramble. Seaview is the island's main second home area for mainlanders, especially Londoners, it is ever so convenient for a quick train and ferry ride from London for the weekend, and it is a good place for boats, so

Cowes Week Sailors from London have homes here, away from the madness of Cowes during that week. Seaview has a few little specialist shops, and a prominent estate agent. They have, or had, a post office, which they were fighting to keep open.

Either way along the coast from Seaview are beautiful walks, the duver to Ryde, or the tidal duver to St. Helens near Bembridge. Duver means sea road or path.

There are hotels on the seafront, and a very nice café which my friends and I often sat outside after a walk from Ryde.

Seaview is a popular sailing village, and you may see boats coming and going, and the dinghy sailing club on their lessons. Nearby is Appley Park, with a lake and play area, and Appley Manor, a grand old stately home that now serves as a hotel and restaurant. There is also tree climbing, archery and camping available in the area. There used to be a much-loved animal park here too, but they had to close down as they couldn't afford to keep running.

Up the hill from Seaview is Nettlestone, a sprawling village with a lot of housing estate running down towards the sea. Nettlestone has a big village green, which has a Christmas tree at Christmas as some of the villages on the island do. There is a shop, an old church and a small plant nursery, but nothing really remarkable about Nettlestone. On the road the other side of the village, towards St. Helens, is a large holiday camp known as 'Nodes Point', overlooking the sea and set out in the countryside, it brings hundreds of people from the mainland every year.

St. Helens is another sprawling village with a large village green, they have a Christmas angels' competition as well as a Christmas tree in December. Angel spotting round the village is fun. St. Helens has several shops, grocery and post office, and a small library. The village greens in St. Helens are extensive and have play areas and sports areas, they add to the charm of the village. There is a road leading back towards Ryde and Brading, and a road that runs down the hill, past exclusive flats and down alongside Bembridge Harbour and those iconic houseboats.

Bembridge and Brading.

Bembridge is very much a sailing town. The road alongside the harbour, heading for the main town. Village (it's called a large village, but it's big enough to be a town), is lined with boat sales places, boat spares and repairs outlets, and boat storage.

On the harbour side of the road are the amazing houseboats, some are permanent or second homes, some are let out or floatels, houseboat hotels.

St. Helens Duver comes round the side of the harbour as a raised path, and the harbour itself is full of boats of all kinds but especially dinghies, as dinghy sailing is big here. It is possible to go through locks and up the river Yar onto the Brading Marshes, but I know very little about that. Only that the marshes are a great wildlife area, RSPB protected, and a great headache to Brading when floods override the flood preventions.

The town of Bembridge is a real community, many people retire there from the mainland, and it has a high population, especially of elderly people, and a cheerful and relaxed atmosphere. There is a library and a church, a village hall and a community centre, shops of all kinds, including a decent chip shop. And on the edge of Brading is the Warner Leisure Hotel that used to allow us from the mere general public in for swimming and bowls.

The Warner Leisure place is alongside Bembridge Bay, where the lifeboat station is open to the public out across a high bridge into the sea, well worth crossing the bridge for the views, and the lifeboat station is a great place to visit when it is open, and you can learn all about the work of the lifeboats. There are also toilets and cafes near the lifeboat station. Bembridge is an unusual bay, Bembridge 'Shelf' is a formation of raised rock that means the sea is shallow for a long way out, and often unwary sailors are grounded here for not realising how shallow the sea is on an ebb, where are their depth calculators? On a low tide this is a good area for low water fishing and treasure hunting. The bay curves round towards Whitecliff bay, the home of the massive holiday park.

One version of the coast path takes you over the fields away from Whitecliff Bay and to Bembridge Windmill, where you can expect to see many tourists from Easter onwards. It gets surprisingly crowded round there. It is a fully intact windmill, of which there are few left in the UK and it is run by the National Trust. It's funny how the proposed wind turbines off the south coast of the island didn't get the same enthusiasm. During the season, you can go up inside the windmill and see its workings, and the view.

Outside of Bembridge there is a small airport, which can confuse people as it is just over the hill from Sandown, which has another small airport. I used to work at the holiday park just by Sandown Airport, you actually have to cross the runway to get to the holiday park.
Above Bembridge Airport is Culver Down, the sheer and steep beauty spot that I mentioned in my walk description.

If you follow the road past Bembridge airport and survive the mad motorists in this area, you cross a small roundabout and head for Brading. You will come out at Yarbridge Cross, where the road runs between Sandown and Brading and the road ahead goes up to the Downs Road. If you want to stop and admire some of the best views of sea and land on the island, go ahead and onto the Downs Road, but mind that the drivers behind you may want to go very fast, and the hill onto the Downs Road is very steep, so choose a low gear.

Before we head for Brading itself, if you turn left at the crossroads and drive a short way, a nondescript little crescent of road on the right will take you to Brading Roman Villa, a family-friendly interactive historic site which is one of the best-preserved Roman villas in the Country, with special mosaics. There is a café, a cinema showing relevant films, and there are guided tours.

Brading, a village set between Ryde, Sandown and Bembridge, is a village with a slight road problem. The speed limit through the village is a strict 20mph, and that is for a good reason. The village road is old and narrow and cannot be widened, the houses along the main road are simply set on the pavement with no garden, the pavements aren't that wide, there is no scope to widen the road, and it is the only road through the village, so when it closes for essential work, as it has done sometimes over the years, or if an accident closes the road, the diversions can be lengthy, back round Bembridge and St. Helens.

Residents get angry with careless driving in the village, and work tirelessly to enforce the speed limit. There is parking at the end of the village towards Ryde, but as with most island car parks, it will cost you. There are or were toilets there too, but as with a lot of public toilets on the island, battles over funding may keep them closed.

The village alongside the road is old and preserved, with some historic architecture, a local museum and doll and toy museum, and an old church dating back to 1100 and in theory open every day, but not always.
Spreading back from the main road are the housing estates that have been built over the years.

Behind the village to one side is the marshland that Brading is known for, controlled by sluices and drains to prevent flooding in the winter, and a site for birdwatching, wildlife, and falling over and getting mucky.

Brading railway station has a platform no longer used for trains with a heritage centre of preserved history of Island Line, and on open days you can enjoy learning to man the signal box as well as learning about the history of the station and line. There is also a tea room there.

Adgestone and Alverstone.

I only mention these as they are hidden gems, shyly hiding in the wooded valleys below the Downs Road between Brading and Sandown. Not many people know about Adgestone and Alvestone. They are pretty villages with small and slow roads, no need to hurry down here. I saw the results of someone trying to be a boy racer down here once as I delivered the early morning papers round the villages. A car, simply run up a bank at a steep angle and sitting in the hedge, abandoned.

There are two focal points down here, one is a very nice holiday camp, very well kept and with great reviews. Sitting peacefully in the countryside on the edge of the village. I would deliver a bundle of papers here during the tourist season, but during the winter they are either closed or very quiet, no papers.

The other place of interest is a Vineyard that is open to the public, the oldest vineyard in the British Isles, Adgestone Vineyard. You can learn about the grapes and wine, try wine tasting and tour the cellars, and there is a café. My social group would go there for lunch sometimes. There are children's activities, animals to meet, live music, and even bed and breakfast accommodation. They are preparing to start doing weddings onsite as well.

The other side of the villages is a lane into Sandown, with a 20mph speed limit. It runs over the river Yar, which sometimes floods and breaches the road. There is also a golf course here.

Island Events.

The island is a sociable and lively place, with civic and social events all the time. Newcomers to the island sometimes see it as a cold place with no social opportunities. Thankfully that impression isn't lasting, you just have to get into island life, and that can take a little while. It helps if you have children, as schools play an active part in island events, and other parents will let you know of things to get involved with.

Although I can't recommend the local weekly paper. The County Press, for accuracy in reporting or ethics, and it is an expensive paper too, it does have a weekly roundup of events and live music for all areas, which is a good way to start off socialising if you move to the island. Local sites such as On the Wight or Wightbay also advertise a selection of events, and Isle of Wight Radio, also a bit hit and miss or selective with reporting, keeps you updated with local events.
There is also a small radio station called Vectis Radio, run by locals from the Riverside Community Centre in Newport, which will keep you updated.
There is a new news site called 'Island Echo' and although they update most local news pretty quickly, they are not very professional and there are many errors on the site. They also tend towards the dramatic or even melodramatic in their sometimes hilariously misspelled stories, for example making *'a boat stuck drifting in the shopping lane of the Solent'* into headlines.
And against islanders wishes and privacy, they for some reason have started publishing court case results, which of course don't tell a full story and are an invasion of privacy in a small community such as the island.

On a typical weekend on the island, there will be car boot sales, jumble sales, garage sales. Art exhibitions, coffee mornings, sponsored events, live music, traffic chaos, and plenty of attractions to visit. You won't be isolated for long if you are a newcomer. And if you prefer peace and quiet, there are simply the downs, the beaches, and many great cafes and restaurants.

There's a walking week, a Randonee, a classic car show, a steam fair, a 'Pirate' week, whatever one of those may be, in fact there are more events than you can possibly attend. There was even a festival of VW Camper Vans and family friendly music and events, but it seems to be on a break.

The Isle of Wight Festival.

The Isle of Wight festival is one of the most famous island events, attracting students, young people and not so young people from the island and around the country as part of the festival season. It is a great event, I would have stewarded there if I hadn't always been so busy with the gardening season.

The Isle of Wight Festival launched in 1968 to 1970 at Freshwater, drawing 600,000 people at the first event, a number of times more people than the population of the island, which seemed to cause great concern and consternation with the authorities, who brought in laws severely restricting festivals. The festival went dormant but was revived in 2002, and has since brought the North of the Island to a standstill every summer as it is located at Seaclose Park on the Newport.

What is the festival like for islanders? Well, some love it, I knew a lady in her sixties who would go down there and dance the night away, but inevitably it causes traffic chaos!

Work on the festival site starts months in advance, huge trucks and lorries, the signing for the 'gates', and the construction of student-proof fencing all round the site, the lighting, the walkways, the stages, the camping areas. Then in the week before the festival, traffic on Fairlee, the main road from Ryde and East Cowes into Newport, goes down to one way and then closes.

When festival goers start arriving, the north of the island becomes traffic jammed chaos and the ferries and mainland travel links become jammed and inaccessible, much to the misery of islanders who have to commute or work in those areas. As a freelancer, I would simply avoid that side of the island and any travel for that time. As with other major events on the island, you have to think and plan ahead to avoid disruption to your life.

I used to work for a property manager, I did his garden and any work needed on his rental properties. He owned a block of flats on Fairlee. One day when I was looking for a new home and working at Fairlee, he showed me round an empty flat in the Fairlee block. It was a bit out of my price range but he said 'You get parking, you are within walking distance to town, and you get free Isle of Wight Festival Tickets'.

The houses in the vicinity of the festival, which is at Seaclose park and on farmland running up Fairlee, get free tickets because of the noise of the festival, which can be heard for miles around but is particularly loud if you live there.

So, residents of Fairlee have it all, despite the road being plagued with congestion and lack of parking for some at other times, and the noise and crowds of the festival being a challenge. They are close enough to town to walk in if the road is closed, they get free tickets for the festival, which can be sold for tidy sums, perfectly legally, and some also sell refreshments and showers to festival goers. No matter how many toilets and showers there are on the festival site, they always get mucky and horrible and with long queues. There are upmarket toilets and showers available there for a significant extra fee but where can you get a nice cup of tea on the festival site? Festival goers also take over the public and supermarket toilets in Newport, leaving locals hopping while they have their washes.

I am not against the festival, anything that does the island good is great, and everyone is having fun, but when you are stuck on an island, things like this can really disrupt life. As I told you, this isn't the glossy tourist guide but the harsh reality one.

The Isle of Wight Festival is coming up to its 50th Anniversary, and was once nearly wiped out by council regulation, which still controls its size. The festival used to have a little rival, over towards Arreton, a similar festival called Bestival, run by hardworking local volunteer Rob de Bank, who is a prominent figure in other island events such as the local Christmas Toy Appeal. Sadly, Bestival left the island and moved to Dorset, and now islanders don't have to plan around the congestion on Arreton Road, closure of the Downs Road and madness on the ferries for that one any more, which is a great shame.

The worst thing was that the area round the main public waste site was inaccessible during Bestival and on a weekend in summer that was outrageous!

Walk the Wight.

Now this is a different walk from my walks round the island. This walk, one Sunday every May, is to raise funds for the local hospice, Mountbatten Hospice. Walk the Wight was a small event originally, but it grew and grew and evolved, drawing every growing crowds of keen walkers from across the UK as well as the island, to walk from Bembridge to Alum bay, a kind of diagonal walk across the island on the downs. On sunny days you get sunburned all down one side.

The main walk is 26 miles, and it is accepted that not everyone can manage this, so there are shorter walks, a flat walk from Sandown to Newport, a schools walk, a half walk, from Newport to Alum Bay. And people can bring their dogs, as long as they register them. Southern Vectis, the local bus service, supports the walk by providing park and ride buses to and from beginnings and ends of walks.

As Walk the Wight is in May, I was always too busy with gardening, however much I tried to find time to go and help or take part, until my last year on the island, when I had to bow out of another event the previous week due to sickness, and thus contacted Walk the Wight to see if I could be a marshal to make up for not helping with the other event. It was so close to the walk that they had a full list of marshals but put me on the reserve list. The day before the walk they contacted me and asked if I could step in due to someone else being ill, and so I marshalled for Walk the Wight.

It was a funny old day, I was caretaking the smallholding and my marshalling duties were due to start at 6am, so I was at the smallholding at 5am to let the animals out and do their feeds and waters. And I was due to go to Wales the next day to house and pet sit for my friends, I was seriously worried that I was overdoing things!

I dashed from the smallholding to the marshalling venue, which was the Isle of Wight College in Newport. I was directed to the head marshal, who was a nice chap but very busy, and he put me on car directing duty and got me a coffee. The college was the park and ride venue for all the walks, so I was to direct cars to spaces as well as directing people to buses, which was interesting as the buses for different walks kept moving around, but there were staff from Southern Vectis standing near the buses, so I directed people to them to direct them to the correct buses. There were the usual people who wouldn't accept car parking directions, you will never marshal at any events without a few like that.
I said that very politely.

I have problems with my legs and spine, and standing still to marshal is not easy for me, so I danced as I directed traffic, so that I could move my legs. This added entertainment for the brave and good people who were heading for the buses in their hundreds to do their long walk. Some said 'You're copying Dancing Jim'! I was really, Dancing Jim is a famous employee of the local ferry, Red Funnel. He directs traffic off the boat by dancing. I am glad that when I left the island he was on duty and I got to say goodbye to him. He always danced and was happy, but he never expected to win an award and a luxury holiday for it when he was voted for in a tourism award.

Anyway, by midday the buses and walkers had all gone and my skills were no longer required, so I went down to Cowes and treated myself to a late breakfast at Eegons and a view of the sailing activities events. I used to sail, I even had a boat, but with a broken spine, I can't use my legs to control a dinghy any more, but I can still watch.

Cowes Week.

Probably the island's most famous event, Cowes Week, the international sailing regatta, with a class for almost every type of boat. Cowes week is when islanders find the little lanes terrorized by big range rovers whose drivers think they own the place.

During Cowes Week, accommodation and dining out is in high demand, the roads are busy, and Cowes is a good place to avoid, unless you live there, but if you live there you can rent your house out for ten days and go on holiday, or rent a room or a driveway out and walk down and join the crowds outside the beer tents to watch the races. Or, of course, you may be out there on the water all week!

As I mentioned previously, I did a lot of sub-contract work around Cowes, as well as caretaking a smallholding at Porchfield. So, I got to meet sailors who were guests on the smallholding accommodation while the owners had sensibly fled the island for the week, and I got to sit on the sea wall at Gurnard and watch the races during my breaks. Of course, it made me miss my sailing days, but I had come to terms with it. It is an amazing sight to see all those races, and you can hear the commentary clearly from Gurnard.

My workmate had once worked nearby for a well-off but disagreeable couple, much like some I have worked for in the past, but when he had enough of poor treatment, he quit. When he quit, the man of the couple threatened to kill him if he ever saw him again.

As we sat on the wall at Gurnard. a boat broke away from the race, coming towards us in the lead. The commentator announced the skipper as being my workmate's former boss who had threatened to kill him.

'He's heading over here, John' I said 'He's seen you!'

Cowes Week involves a lot of drinking and celebration, and ends in a huge firework display. Crowds pack the seafront at Cowes and Gurnard. And the Red Arrows mooch thoughtfully past. There are opportunities to go out on one of the ferries for a fireworks cruise. I did this once, to evaluate the experience for a book I hoped to write one day, a book about the island. I wonder if I will ever write it?

The fireworks cruise wasn't well advertised, I heard someone mutter about it on Isle of Wight Radio or Wave 105, as a cruise was being run from Southampton as well as from East Cowes.

I had to scramble about on the website just to find it. It was a rather badly co-ordinated setup, I was told when I inquired that I could leave my car in Ryde and get a complimentary coach which would come from Sandown and Bembridge, and there would be other coaches.

But there wasn't a coach in the end. There must have been enough parking in East Cowes for most who got through the traffic early enough, because the organizers cancelled our coach and sent a taxi. There were two other locals and two tourist couples, and we all fitted in a big taxi. But there was confusion about the return transport and the driver phoned in and was reassured that return transport was booked...as islanders would say 'Ha!'.

East Cowes was crowded with people waiting for the cruise who had not booked transport. I was sure I should have just driven to Whippingham and walked down. We saw a bit of the Red Arrows through the clouds while we were stuck in traffic in the taxi.

Now it was getting dark, and the loading of people onto the ferries was chaotic, I briefly saw people I knew as we were herded up and down, and just by a fluke I ended up as the first person to board due to being in the right place at the right time. I was so puzzled and I looked back and everyone was following me. On board there was tea and refreshments, for a fee of course, there was also live music. I got a cuppa and went out on deck, only because it wasn't a normal ferry run, we were allowed on the car decks. It felt funny to walk around the car deck as I videoed the flotsam of boats out on the water. The boats were all lighting up now, and among them the blue lights of police and patrol boats flashed, while on the shore the lights of glow sticks and wheels sparkled among the crowds at Gurnard.

We passed other cruise boats, mainly from Southampton, everyone waving and laughing, and a boat with a Scottish Piper, complete with kilt, came alongside us and serenaded us. I was glad it wasn't windy.

We cruised a long way out towards Yarmouth, allowing the normal service passenger ferries to avoid the boats and go into the Medina. We turned and came alongside the sister ship from Southampton and the two ferries side by side moved back up towards Gurnard and the Medina without disrupting any boats. A paddle steamer, which may have been the local hero, the Waverly, was nearby and sang out a very rattly and humorous horn blast.

Blasts on horns started, and the big horns signalled the start of the fireworks, and it was a great display. Out there on the water we got the perfect view of the fireworks, and I got them on video, while still enjoying my cup of tea.

We had been told we would be in dock again by 10.30, but due to water traffic as hundreds of boats started to leave the island, it was an hour later and we had to sail back up towards the West Wight while we waited.

When we got in dock, there was no taxi for us, there was a coach but that was for Sandown only and the driver said he wasn't allowed to take us. When someone phoned the taxi company, they were told that our taxi had been told to arrive at 9.30, did so, thought we were ferry passengers, found no one there and headed for Cowes where there was loads of work. The co-ordinators had totally failed us, and the taxi firms were fully booked with Cowes Week customers all night. A few angry phone calls later we were told that a taxi would be there as soon as possible. It was nearly midnight now, and one couple, in desperation, caught the last number five bus up to racecourse to change and get the nine back to Ryde, while rest of us waited and fumed. I had the smallholding to look after before my other work in the morning, so the last thing I needed was a late night.

The taxi driver was confused about what had happened, he had been shuffled from another job. So the others explained the situation and he was a bit horrified that we had been stranded. He dropped us in Ryde and we said goodnight and headed our separate ways.
   As I went through Ryde, two people chased a man over the road and started beating him up, I was going to intervene as I didn't know what to do, but a Southern Vectis bus came round the corner and would have caught them on dashcam. So they stopped fighting. But the next day when the police appealed for witnesses, I let them know I was a witness, and would you believe it? They never got back in touch. Maybe the bus CCTV was enough.
   The fireworks cruise was certainly interesting, but I would never do it again, and I was refunded some money because of the transport mess-up.

The Scooter Rally.

Imagine thousands of scooters, many covered in lamps or wing mirrors and some with bikes or riders dressed up. Imagine these scooters careering round the roads of the island and congregating in great groups by cafes and on seafronts. That is what the Isle of Wight Scooter Rally looks like. The rally draws scooters from all over the country and even from Europe.

The Scooter Rally is held on the bank holiday weekend in August, and is cursed by grumpy old locals for being another traffic disruption, but is tolerated with good humour by those of us who see the good it does to the island and the local economy.

The scooters gather at Ryde, where there will be live music, plenty of beer and entertainment, and a great social experience for riders, as well as locals who come to admire the scooters. There are ride-outs from Ryde, planned ones and small individual groups, and while traffic can be slowed as a result, it is such fun. Sandown also gets a major planned Scooter ride-out, they go along the seafront and through the town, and the residents turn out in force to see them. I remember doing a video of this ride-out some years ago, but sadly I have neither the videos nor any pictures to share as they were lost.
As with all big events, the volume of riders and scooters affects the ferries and can make travel difficult, as well as affecting the road.

Ryde Pride and Slide.

Pride is a relatively new event to Ryde and the island, and the Slide was there first and a separate event. Both are in the summer and have now merged to make a weekend event.
Ryde Slide is a massive water slide down the hill on Union Street in Ryde, on the road, it is a charity fundraiser, with the local fire crew very much involved. The Slide closes the road, and is thus another traffic problem to drive the locals mad. You have to book in advance if you want to slide down Ryde on a water slide, as the event is extremely popular and gets fully booked.

Ryde Pride has been running for a few years and was originally a separate event from the slide, but the decision was made to have them on the same weekend and close the road for two days. Pride is an event for everyone, there is a huge parade through town, and almost everyone I know, friends, families, straight or gay, go and enjoy this if they aren't busy working. Pride has a great atmosphere and reportedly great beer. Unfortunately I managed to miss it both years due to work. It's a whole weekend of partying, but if you live outside Ryde, then you will have to allow plenty of time to get through the traffic jams and find somewhere to park!

In 2018, Ryde hosted European Pride, so it became not just local, not just national, but international, and that was obviously great. I was working and couldn't make it, and my housemates, a lovely gay couple, were also working and couldn't make it.

I was horrified to attend a church service just before Pride, and hear an openly homophobic sermon condemning Pride and gay people. I wrote to the church leaders, but they didn't reply, and so I didn't attend that church again. Jesus said 'Judge Not' and he said 'Love your neighbour as yourself'. And never did he say discriminate. I hope that my views do not offend you.

Garlic Festival.

As already mentioned, this wonderful festival of garlic, entertainment and live music is run by the Garlic Farm, and they have every kind of garlic and every possible recipe, as well as loads of other stalls and crafts. This is the festival that causes chaos on the Arreton Road now that Bestival no longer does. Get there early, be prepared for delays and ask them if they can get the Wurzels back again for another year.

Sandown and Shanklin Regatta.

There will always be fog, rough seas or unwanted weather for this rowing race between Shanklin and Sandown piers in the summer, so get used to it.

The Carnivals.

The island is big on carnivals and they aren't all a disaster like the one I mentioned marshalling for. Sandown is my personal favourite, it is a big one, well-coordinated and very professionally put together. The roads close (guess what, it causes traffic problems!). The Carnival Queens and other royalty are there early, on their float down on the seafront. The floats gather on the seafront, and you can walk along, view them, and get pictures. The participants and queens are usually happy to be photographed and will wave and smile for you. The parade goes from the seafront through the high street and down the back roads in a big loop back to Fort Street and the seafront. The crowds are huge, there are glow sticks, refreshments, whistles. It is a lovely atmosphere. And the other towns have similar, including the road closures.

In the autumn and winter, the same floats and people gather for the illuminated carnivals, with the floats lit up in the evening. Sandown's tends to be at the end of October or beginning of November and ends in a spectacular firework display out on the sea, literally, the fireworks are staged on ropes out over the sea, and everyone gathers on the beach and front to watch these fireworks go up from the sea in the dark. Really special.

Newport's illuminated carnival is combined with the grand Christmas lights switch-on some weeks later. I have to say it isn't as grand as Sandown's illuminated carnival, but the traffic chaos it causes is impressive. Imagine you are a delivery driver trying to get round Newport with a load of roads closed. It is very difficult.

Jack up the 80s and Fairweather Festival.

Jack up the 80s is an established 80s music festival at Smallbrook Stadium in Ryde in association with Jack FM, very popular and very loud. I know a certain person who was a hard worker and didn't go out much to events, but he would never miss Jack up the 80s, he would be out for the weekend, enjoying the music and the beer, and he would still come to work on Monday, with a sore head and a long face, but he loved that festival.
In 2019, Jack up the 80s will move from Ryde to North Fairlee Farm where the Isle of Wight Festival is held, and will be renamed 'Jack up the Summer', with a smaller weekend offshoot event being planned for a different date.

Fairweather Festival is a bit of a meaningless money-spinner that appears to have been created and marketed by Island Echo. It doesn't seem to have a reason or meaning, except to cause traffic chaos in Sandown, where it is held at Los Altos Park. It is music and entertainment, making the most of the summer holidays, I guess. I was surprised when they had the Chuckle

Brothers there, and by that time, the younger Chuckle must have already known he had cancer, I think he died before the next festival. I always liked the Chuckle Brothers. RIP Paul.

The Round the Island Race.

A big boat race that starts very early from Cowes and goes round the island anti-clockwise. You can view it from anywhere but there are good viewing points, for example, the military road cliffs and Ventnor cliffs, Chale church opens its tower to viewers, Ryde pier is a good place in the afternoon to watch them coming in, and Bembridge cliffs is also a good viewpoint. And if you feel like it, you can always book yourself a place on a race boat, for a fee, this is easy if you belong to local sailing clubs, a bit trickier otherwise. I used to get invites to race, but my sailing days were really over by the time I lived on the Isle of Wight.

The Old Gaffers.

This was a bi-yearly regatta for old wooden-built gaff-rigged boats, known as gaffers. There have been issues about funding and managing this event, which is held at Yarmouth. There used to be a big market and lots of entertainment, a marching band, classic cars, and refreshments, but that was all stopped, as far as I last heard. I did help out there, on the market bit, hard work but lots of food. The boats look amazing fully dressed out and it was a lovely day for the town so I hope it can be continued.

The Jazz Weekend.

Once a year, in the summer, the jazz comes to town. But it isn't a big one-place event like the Isle of Wight Festival, the jazz festival is a schedule of events in pubs, clubs and other venues around the town and island. It used to be the Jazz Festival, based in Ventnor but has changed, to be around Newport for a weekend.

Rhythm Tree Festival.

A big family friendly festival with camping and a cafe. Diverse music and singing, exhibitions, and individual practitioners of things such as reiki, yoga, meditation and similar mind-body exercises as well as craft stalls. The festival is ethically run and aimed to be good for wellbeing. It takes place in the summer on a farm between Calbourn and Shalfleet.

The swims.

The Boxing Day Swim at Ventnor to raise money for local families receiving medical treatment on the mainland.
There is also a Shanklin Pier to Sandown Pier swim at some point in the year, to raise money for the lifeboats.

Other events.

Island attractions have a schedule of events all year round. The steam railway is the solid eventer, they never get tired of new events to draw people in. Alum Bay, Osbourn House, Blackgang Chine, the Donkey Sanctuary and others have a regular schedule of events. There are also schools' events, sea events, Armed Forces and Memorial events, there is a walking week in which many visitors explore the island on foot as I used to. The Isle of Wight is never boring. There is always something going on. The Isle of Wight is a community, and each town and village is a community within it.

Boat Trips.

The island offers numerous boat and fishing trips, mainly from Cowes or Yarmouth. You can enjoy the views of the island from the outside, learn a bit of sea fishing or go on a fast RIB ride that will leave your heart pounding. At the weekend, day boat trips to Portsmouth are available for shopping, at a reasonable price, but spaces are limited.
One of the most popular and quickly booked trips is a trip round the island on the Waverly paddle steamer, a preserved and running paddle steamer that is well-known locally. On the Waverly you can enjoy a blend of history in travelling on a real working paddle steamer, while also taking in the amazing views of the outside of the island, all you need is good weather for the day.

Island Activities.

There are many sports and outdoors activities available on the island, and being an island, there are sea-based activities as well. Sea activities include sailing training, at Sandown, Yaverland, Bembridge and Cowes among others, kayaking, surf school and paddle boarding.
On Sandown revetment, you can hire dinghies, kayaks, surf and paddle boards. There are surf schools which train at Compton Bay and sometimes at Sandown.
Shanklin, Cowes and Ryde have accredited rowing clubs. But don't contact the Shanklin one through the website form, as they never answer.

Other activities include tree climbing at Ryde, guided walks, fossil hunts, go-karting, fishing and fishing lessons, both sea and lake based, archery (near Ryde), cycling, horse riding, and more. There are running activities based at the stadium behind Sandown Bay Academy (High School). The running track there is designed for professional running as it is used for the Island Games running events.
(Island Games are where islands round the world compete in sports, the UK's Channel Islands, Isle of Wight and Isle of Man take part).

If you like music, the island has several brass bands that you can join and receive training. Shanklin has a brass band which performs at events and ceremonies, but they ignore email enquiries, and there is also Vectis Brass Band, who are the better-known band, often seen at civic events and carnivals.

These activities are easily looked up, so I won't bore you with endless details. The Website 'On the Wight' is a very useful source of island information and activities of all kinds and I can recommend it. There are events and clubs of every kind, for everyone. Being an island doesn't mean being socially backward as some mainlanders assume.

Now a small voice asks if there is any nightlife in Newport or the island. Well, yes, it's a small place and so there are a few clubs, a few pubs, a bit of noise and drinking. It isn't devoid of nightlife, it's just that I am not a pub or club person.

Newport, and other towns, have a good selection of live music at pubs and restaurants, and a lot of local artists.

There are night buses at the weekend and mainlanders come over for a pub crawl, so there must be some night life. There's a good cinema that also does National Theatre Live productions, (which is my idea of a night out), there are plenty of restaurants, pizza hut at the cinema, and next door to the cinema is one of the pubs where you can start your nightlife stuff, the Man in the Moon pub.

I have heard of three night clubs, 'Fever' and 'Envy' in Newport, and 'Colonel Bogeys' in Sandown. I can't say much more as I have never gone out for 'nightlife' or drinking. My version of a night out is a meal in a pub or restaurant with friends or a trip to cinema or theatre, which goes on too late for me by 10 or 11pm. The island has a lot of good pubs and restaurants. I am sure you can find nightlife if you look hard enough.

Conclusion.

It was nice to be able to re-explore the island through this short book, I hope that you have enjoyed it, and I hope that your experience of the island is good. For all its problems, it is beautiful and diverse place, with attractions for everyone.

I finish this book at 10.30pm on December 29th, 2018, less than a week after I started writing it. And now I will go to bed and maybe dream of my island, as I often do. Sandown bay in the golden sun, but more often Newport's dark streets in winter. I loved the island in winter, when all the visitors had gone home, and it was ours again, there was space to walk and dream like Tennyson did, and as I did on that first Great Walk, which made the island my home.

This book is for everyone who might fall in love with the island, and also for me, to keep with me and keep my memory of the island alive until I come back.

Printed in Great
Britain
by Amazon